HOW TO EAT **OUTSIDE**

www.transworldbooks.co.uk

HOW TO EAT
OUTSIDE

Fabulous Al Fresco Food for BBQs, Bonfires,
Camping and More

GENEVIEVE TAYLOR

BANTAM PRESS

LONDON · TORONTO · SYDNEY · AUCKLAND · JOHANNESBURG

Contents

INTRODUCTION

This book started with a hunch, and the hunch was this: if you think of the most memorable meals of your life, then I bet many, if not most of them, have been eaten outside. A little poll of friends and family backed me up on the idea that, as a nation, we have an enduring love for 'al fresco'. And so *How to Eat Outside* was born.

For me, food – good, simple, un-mucked-about-with food – is absolutely central to life's pleasures and despite the inevitable struggles with the weather, there is no getting away from the fact that food simply tastes better when eaten out of doors. I wonder if part of the joy is that, because our weather can be a challenge, food eaten outside can feel a bit like a holiday and an energizing break from the routine, and yet it's such an easy thing to do. Not just limited to what tasty things you're putting in your mouth, I think the pleasure stems also from the surroundings, the company you are with and perhaps even the fresh air you're taking in as you eat. It all adds up to a winning combination. With a lifelong love affair with the great outdoors, there's nothing I like better than rustling up something delicious for an al fresco adventure.

There are many amazing outside meals that will remain lodged in my memory for years to come and, I might add, they are not *always* those I have eaten in the hazy sun of midsummer. As a family we eat outside at every possible opportunity during spring, summer and well into the autumn. It's not unheard of in winter either, and providing we can find a little shelter on a crisp sunny day, or some warmth from a roaring fire in the garden, it's often a surprisingly lovely thing to do.

Probably the best sausage sandwich of my life was gobbled greedily on a damp mossy bank next to a wild Welsh waterfall. Cooking in the shelter of a large oak tree, we just about managed to keep the stove alight in the wind and drizzle, but the resulting crispy fried bangers tasted simply phenomenal shoved into hunks of French bread. Simple food, an amazing setting and a hunger fuelled by the efforts of the walk to get there all added up to a perfect meal. Another more recent edible highlight was a long lazy lunch in the garden feasting on barbecued fish and a salad of home-grown figs, fresh herbs and creamy ricotta, the rare day of scorching summer sun tempered by plenty of chilled wine. This is the food I will continue to remember many years after I ate it.

Giving yourself, your family and your friends some amazing food memories they will treasure for years is not about feeding them show-off, trying-too-hard food. In fact, in my world it is quite the opposite. It's about taking a few fresh ingredients and treating them with a little bit of love and a big hit of flavour. For this reason, herbs and spices should be your best friends in the kitchen, whether that kitchen is inside or out, and I urge you to use them both daily and generously.

The food in this book is aimed at people, with or without kids, who like to cook and eat just a little adventurously. My children, aged 10 and 7, are not yet the most courageous of eaters, inherently suspicious of new things, but little by

little I try to broaden their horizons. To my delight, my son said the other day that the drawer full of spices was his favourite drawer in the kitchen because it smelt so nice when he opened it. Since he was very small I have tried to get him to help me select which spices to use, letting him take the lids off jars to have a lingering sniff of this and that. He still may not eat all the things I offer him but I hope that slowly, slowly the tactic is working.

Getting my kids involved in the cooking process is without a doubt helping them to get interested in creating food for themselves. By turning the process of cooking into an adventure, by cooking and eating it together in the big outdoors, whether that's in your back garden or further afield, it becomes not just fuel but a celebration of simple pleasures.

How to Eat Outside is split into five chapters, each becoming a little less connected to your home surroundings as you delve further through the book. Picnics and barbecues are probably what spring to mind first when you think of al fresco eating, but what about cooking over a bonfire or an open fire in the autumn, or taking your family camping for a long weekend by the beach? And for the ultimate outdoor eating experience, you can't beat a bit of mountainside cooking to rejuvenate body and soul. I have chosen to put certain recipes into certain chapters principally because those were the occasions that I cooked them for. However, many recipes could easily straddle two or even more chapters. It is my hope that you will use my ideas as a guide for shaping your own outside feasts, whatever the occasion or location.

There's no doubt that warmth is a bonus, and if it can't come in the form of sunshine and endless balmy evenings, then a roaring campfire comes a pretty close second. To cook well in the outdoors, a few bits of simple kit are invaluable and you'll find details of the things I like to use at the start of each chapter. Not an enormous gadget fan, I try to keep equipment to a minimum, but there are definitely a few things I wouldn't dream of giving up now I've got used to using them. For wild adventures, my Trangia storm cooker has proved invaluable as a super portable cook-anywhere stove. Otherwise, my principal tools are my fire pit and tripod with its barbecue grill, and my Dutch oven. During the writing of this book, they have seen many, many evenings of fun and seriously nice food and I hope you'll be amazed by the edible delights that it's possible to create over an open fire.

Whether you are looking for a few tasty things to take on a lazy-day picnic, easy food for a relaxed garden barbecue, some warming treats for a bonfire night celebration or camping trip, or something hale and hearty to sustain you on a mountain hike, *How to Eat Outside* is the fresh-air-lover's cookery bible, packed full of great ideas and delicious recipes for year-round al fresco feasting.

PACK UP A
PICNIC

Introduction

Most of us truly love the *idea* of a picnic and that perfectly hazy idyll of rose-tinted childhood memories, a rug spread with edible goodies stretched out along a river bank, or a basket laden with delicious treats driven out to the countryside for a ramble. But it's not just lazy summer outings when it is useful to have delicious on-the-go food to hand.

Possibly the worst meal I ever ate was a foul pie at an arctic-cold football match. How much nicer would it have been to munch on a home-made pasty discreetly slipped from inside my jacket pocket? Just as with my footie pie, a picnic feast can often, sadly, be a real disappointment – squashed sandwiches with bread soft and slimy from a too-wet filling, or limp salad that has slid around for way too long in a watery dressing.

By its very nature picnic food needs to be eminently transportable, so robust pies and bakes are ideal, as are interesting fillings for DIY sarnies, and salads that mature gracefully rather than wilt miserably.

If I were to offer one top tip, it would be to keep it simple and do a few things well rather than strive for an endless picnic basket with masses of variety. I think the art to choosing the food you take lies in selecting things that taste as nice, if not better, eaten at room temperature rather than either piping hot or fridge cold.

Perhaps you are looking to pack up a picnic for a day at the races, or for a more elaborate feast at an outdoor concert or theatre performance. Maybe you want to provide that all-elusive perfect picnic spread for a family outing, or a tasty pocketable snack to fuel you at a sporting event, or (my favourite) you simply want to grab a blanket and a couple of cushions and set up camp in the garden. All these different picnic styles require a slightly different approach to eating.

Think of a picnic as a small transportable party where ultimately 'party'-type food will work best. So finger food, or at the very most a one-handed fork feast, is your best bet. Bring a knife into the equation and it all gets a bit too much. The ultimate travelling picnic needs something you can wrap and pocket. One or two tubs in a rucksack is fine if you're walking, or if you're not going too far from the car, a quiche or a whole cake protected in a tin or an old-fashioned picnic basket can provide a slightly more luxurious spread.

Of course the weather is not always as kind as we might like, but that doesn't necessarily mean it needs to stop the party. The boot of an estate car, or the back of a van if you're lucky enough to have one, makes for a great al-fresco-ish venue. I think there's something wonderful about being within a whisper of the elements yet sheltered enough to be cosy. In a full-on gale, a picnic on the (well-protected!) carpet in the front room can be a hoot, especially for young kids, and a grown-up bed picnic on a rainy day can be a joy.

This chapter includes a multitude of exciting and delicious dishes that will travel well with both ease and style and will truly satisfy those hunger pangs, whatever your picnicking occasion.

EQUIPMENT RULES

Whilst you don't really *need* any special equipment to enjoy a picnic – at its minimal best, a pocket in which to carry something to eat is sufficient – depending on the venue, you may want to up the sense of occasion with a wicker picnic basket or proper crockery. For example, on the rare occasion that I have gone to an outside theatre production armed with a nice bottle of wine, I wouldn't dream of drinking it out of anything other than real glasses. I'd rather open a can of coke than drink wine out of plastic cups.

If you're eating more than a simple hand-held snack, you will need something both to sit on and to spread your food out on – I find a waterproof coat is pretty adequate most of the time, or one of those roll-up travel rugs is great too. Conversely, you wouldn't want to spread out a rug and open up a fancy hamper if you were watching a rugby match or, for that matter, carry it all on a long walk – that's when pockets or rucksacks and plastic tubs are useful. Simply put, your picnicking equipment should match your picnic aspirations.

A FEW QUICK, ALMOST INSTANT, IDEAS...

Some of my most memorable picnics have been the ones where the food wasn't over-thought about or fussy, on days that started with a dawn so glorious that I didn't want to miss a minute of fun. Here are a few almost instant ideas for impromptu picnics:

- **Crisp butties** – cheap crisps, your favourite flavour, plus white bread, ready-buttered. When you get to where you're going, open up your bread, open up your crisps, stuff the crisps inside the bread and tuck in.

- **Hard-boiled eggs** – cooked, cooled and transported in their shells, hard-boiled eggs are robust and protected and they make perfectly neat little picnic packages. I usually take a mini foil twist of salt and black pepper along too, perhaps flavoured with a few spices (cumin and dried chilli flakes are ideal) to dunk them in as I eat.

- **A simple ploughman's on the go** – for a very easy low-faff picnic, you can't beat a fresh French loaf that can be torn greedily, some perfect cheese and perhaps a little ham or salami, plus a few cherry tomatoes on the vine. Soft cheeses like Brie, Camembert or Cambazola are great for picnics as they ooze lusciously when out of the fridge, rather than break out into a sulky sweat like a Cheddar would.

- **A tin of tuna** – on an Italian beach a long time ago, I clearly remember wrestling with the tin opener on my penknife, trying to make headway into a tin of tuna. The resulting oily, sandy sandwich was memorable for all the wrong reasons! Thankfully these days you can buy tinned tuna packed in good olive oil with an easy access ring pull, that makes for a delicious instant lunch when tipped into a crusty bread roll.

Picnic flat bread

Whilst buying a crusty loaf to take on your picnic is undoubtedly the quicker option, there is much satisfaction to be had from a bit of stress-busting kneading when making your own loaf. This flat bread is designed to be torn apart and shared (I see little point in taking a rather cumbersome bread knife on a picnic). I like to add the wholemeal flour for the extra texture it gives, but use all white if you'd rather.

MAKES 2 FLAT LOAVES (EACH LOAF SERVES 3–4)

1 tsp dried yeast
1 tsp caster sugar
About 550ml hand-hot water
650g strong white bread flour, plus extra for dusting
150g strong wholemeal bread flour

1 tsp fine sea salt
3 tbsp olive oil, plus extra for greasing, kneading and drizzling
3 cloves garlic, thinly sliced
3–4 sprigs of rosemary, leaves picked
Sea salt flakes, for sprinkling

Grease and lightly flour 2 baking sheets.

Add the yeast and sugar to a jug and pour over 100ml of the hand-hot water, stirring well until dissolved. Set aside for 10 minutes or so until you see little foamy bubbles on the surface.

Weigh the flours into a mixing bowl, add the fine sea salt and mix. Pour in the measured oil and the yeasty water, adding another 400ml of the hand-hot water as well. Use a wooden spoon to bring the dough together. Add a little more warm water if necessary to incorporate all the flour – it should be pretty soft, but not overly sticky.

Drizzle a little oil on to a clean worktop and spread it around with your hands. Tip the rough dough on to it and knead well until the dough is smooth and stretchy, about 5–8 minutes.

Cut the dough in half and place each in the centre of a prepared baking sheet. Use your hands to pat and stretch out each piece to a flat loaf about 1cm thick. Make deep dimples in the dough with your fingers, then press the garlic and rosemary into the holes. Drizzle over a little extra oil and add a sprinkle of sea salt flakes. Cover with a clean tea towel and leave to rise on the worktop for 30 minutes.

Preheat the oven to 220°C/Gas 7.

Bake the flat breads in the oven for around 15–20 minutes until golden and baked through.

And three easy spreadables to eat with the flat bread...

I like to make these quick and tasty pâtés in a food processor so they are smooth, but make them by hand with a masher or fork for a coarser texture, if you prefer.

Each pâté will serve around 4, and I might be tempted to make them all, since they are so straightforward. They will all keep for up to 3 days in the fridge.

Ricotta, pea and lemon pâté

250g frozen peas
1 x 250g tub ricotta
Finely grated zest and juice of about
   ½ lemon, or to taste

Sea salt and freshly ground black pepper

Plunge the peas into a pan of boiling water and cook for 3 minutes. Drain well, then simply process or mash them with the ricotta and lemon in a bowl to achieve the desired consistency. Season to taste with salt and black pepper, then cover and chill in the fridge until needed.

Easy smoked mackerel and horseradish pâté

1 x 200g tub cream cheese
   (full-fat or light, as you wish)
170g smoked mackerel fillets,
   skinned and flaked

1–2 tsp horseradish sauce, or to taste
Small bunch of chives, snipped
Sea salt and freshly ground black pepper

Simply mix everything together, either in a bowl, or by whizzing in a food processor. Season to taste with salt and black pepper, adding a little more horseradish for extra bite, if you like. Cover and chill in the fridge until needed.

Moroccan-spiced carrot and butter bean 'hummus'

500g carrots (about 4 large ones), peeled
   and sliced
3 tbsp olive oil
1 clove garlic, crushed
1 tsp *each* cumin and coriander seeds,
   roughly ground
½–1 tsp dried chilli flakes, or to taste

1 x 400g tin butter beans, drained and
   rinsed
Small bunch of coriander, chopped
1–2 tsp white wine vinegar or sherry
   vinegar, or to taste
Sea salt and freshly ground black pepper

Cook the carrots in a pan of boiling water until just tender, about 15 minutes. Drain and then whilst they are still hot, mix in the oil, garlic and spices.

If you are using a food processor, tip the mixture in, add the butter beans and chopped coriander and whizz to a purée, adding a splash of water if necessary to help it along. Season to taste with salt and black pepper, then sharpen with a little vinegar. Alternatively, mash the cooked carrots with the rest of the ingredients.

Scoop into a bowl and leave to cool, then cover and chill in the fridge until needed.

picnic-friendly salads

Not all salads are created equal when it comes to picnics. You need something that will travel well and here are two of my favourites. There are also a few great on-the-move salads to be found in the Barbecue Feast and Wilderness Eats chapters.

Italian-style potato salad

This is a salad that I make often, ideal for all manner of al fresco events, as it contains no mayo and only improves by sitting around a bit. It's a great one for barbecues too (see photo on page 55).

SERVES 4–6

750g new potatoes, halved
4 tbsp extra virgin olive oil
2 tbsp balsamic vinegar
1 tbsp Dijon mustard
1 red onion, finely chopped

Large bunch of basil, roughly chopped
1 clove garlic, crushed
1 tsp caster sugar
Sea salt and freshly ground black pepper

Put the potatoes in a pan of cold water, add a shake of salt and bring to the boil. Simmer for 15 minutes or so until just tender.

Meanwhile, in a small bowl, whisk together the oil, vinegar, mustard, onion, basil, garlic and sugar, adding a little salt and plenty of black pepper.

Drain the potatoes well, then stir through the dressing whilst they are hot. Leave to cool to room temperature before serving – the dressing will soak in and flavour the potatoes beautifully.

Asian-style slaw with peanuts, lime and sesame oil

Coleslaw with an irresistible Asian zing, this is hot, sharp and sweet. It also keeps really well in the fridge, so is a good one to make ahead of time. (See photo on page 27.)

SERVES 4–6

400g red cabbage, finely shredded
1 red pepper, deseeded and finely sliced
Bunch of spring onions, chopped
½ cucumber, cut into matchsticks
Handful *each* of coriander and mint,
   roughly chopped

2 tbsp *each* soy sauce and sesame oil
1 tbsp *each* runny honey and fish sauce
Finely grated zest and juice of 2 limes
1–2 bird's eye chillies, finely chopped
1 clove garlic, crushed

Mix together the cabbage, red pepper, spring onions, cucumber and herbs in a large bowl. In a small bowl or jug, whisk together the soy sauce, oil, honey, fish sauce, lime zest and juice, chillies and garlic.

Pour the dressing over the salad and toss to mix. Serve immediately or cover and chill in the fridge for up to 3 days.

a couple of tasty tarts for sharing

Tarts are great for a picnic, especially if you transport them in the tin so they are robustly packaged. I usually make my own pastry for quiches but, of course, the ready-made stuff is perfectly acceptable too, especially if you buy all-butter pastry. About half a 500g pack is what you'll need to line the tin.

Smoked trout, watercress and horseradish quiche

MAKES A 25CM QUICHE/SERVES 4-ISH

For the pastry
180g plain flour, plus extra for dusting
A pinch of fine sea salt
90g cold butter, diced
3–4 tbsp ice-cold water

For the filling
1 tbsp olive oil
1 onion, finely chopped
1 x 110g bag watercress, roughly chopped
2 tbsp horseradish sauce
2 skinless smoked trout fillets (about
    125g in total), roughly flaked
3 eggs
250g crème fraîche
Sea salt and freshly ground black pepper

To make the pastry, put the flour, salt and butter into a food processor and pulse together until the mixture resembles coarse breadcrumbs. Trickle in the water, continuing to pulse, until the pastry just starts to clump together (don't over-process or the pastry can become tough). Tip on to a sheet of cling film and gently press into a ball. Wrap tightly and chill in the fridge for at least 30 minutes before rolling.

Meanwhile, prepare the filling. Heat the oil in a large frying pan and gently sweat the onion until soft, about 15–20 minutes. Add the watercress and let it wilt for a couple of minutes, then remove from the heat and leave to cool.

Preheat the oven to 200°C/Gas 6.

Roll out the pastry on a lightly floured worktop to about 3–4mm thick and use it to line a 25cm loose-based tart tin (trying not to stretch it too much), then swiftly roll the rolling pin over the top of the tin, cutting off the excess pastry. Line with non-stick baking paper and fill with baking beans. Bake in the oven for 20 minutes. Remove the paper and beans and bake for a further 5 minutes to dry out.

Spread the horseradish sauce over the base of the cooked pastry case, then spoon in the watercress mixture. Scatter the trout over the top. In a jug, beat together the eggs and crème fraîche and season well with salt and black pepper, before gently pouring over the filling. Return to the oven to cook for about 20 minutes until set. Leave to cool completely before wrapping ready for your picnic basket.

Caramelized garlic, spinach and mushroom tart

The inspiration for this rich vegetarian tart came from a delicious Ottolenghi recipe in his *Plenty* cookbook. The blanching and caramelizing really mellows the garlic so don't worry about it being too pungent.

MAKES A 25CM QUICHE/SERVES 4-ISH

1 x 25cm blind-baked pastry case (as per quiche recipe on page 18)
2 whole heads of garlic, cloves separated
2 tbsp olive oil
2 tbsp balsamic vinegar
1 tsp caster sugar
125g chestnut mushrooms, thickly sliced

2 sprigs of thyme, leaves picked
250g spinach, washed and well dried (preferably spun in a salad spinner)
300ml single cream
2 large eggs
Sea salt and freshly ground black pepper

Make and blind-bake the pastry case as directed in the quiche recipe on page 18 (preheating the oven to 200°C/Gas 6, when required).

Meanwhile, add the unpeeled garlic cloves to a large saucepan and pour over just enough boiling water to cover. Set over a high heat and blanch for 5 minutes. Drain, then cool a little so you can squeeze the cloves from their skins. They should pop out very easily.

Return the pan to the hob and set over a very low heat. Add the oil, vinegar, sugar and peeled garlic cloves and leave to caramelize for around 10 minutes. Shake the pan every now and then to stop it sticking. Stir through the mushrooms and thyme, increase the heat a little and fry for about 10 minutes, until they have released and reabsorbed their liquid – they should become quite dry. Add the spinach, cover and let it wilt for a couple of minutes, stirring once to help it along.

In a jug, lightly whisk the cream and eggs together with a fork. Season with salt and plenty of black pepper. Spoon the vegetables into the cooked pastry case, then gently pour over the egg mixture.

Bake in the oven for 25 minutes until just set. Leave to cool to room temperature before packing for your picnic.

Some other ideas...

There are many ways to change a tart, and there are no hard and fast rules, which is why they are so useful to make. For each pastry case allow 2–3 eggs and around 250–300ml cream or crème fraîche (or even milk for a slightly less rich version) to make the custard base. Basically, the more 'bits' you add to the filling, the less custard base you need, and as a general rule the bits should be lightly cooked before adding to the quiche. Here are a few of my most loved combinations:

- Caramelized red onion, purple sprouting broccoli and Brie

- Leek, blue cheese and walnut

- Crab and asparagus (use an equal mix of white and brown crab meat for the best flavour)

individual picnic bakes

Whilst a cuttable quiche for sharing is a very lovely thing, there is also something rather nice about having an individual pie just for one. The practicality of not having to take a knife is one very good reason, but it also feels kind of special to be offered a pie just for yourself.

Bombay spiced beef and potato pasties

I love a pasty as much as the next person and hailing from Cornwall I should probably think of this recipe as sacrilege. But I'm also a fiend for spices and can rarely resist adding them to liven up my cooking. These pasties (see photo on page 35) are great served with mango chutney, or try them with the Fiery Carrot Pickle on page 34.

MAKES 6 PASTIES

1 x 500g pack ready-made puff pastry
   (ideally the all-butter variety)
Plain flour, for dusting
1 egg, beaten, to glaze

For the filling
500g potatoes, peeled and cut into
   1cm cubes

250g minced beef
1 large onion, finely chopped
2 cloves garlic, crushed
50g butter, melted
2 tbsp mustard seeds
1 tsp ground turmeric
Small bunch of coriander, chopped
Sea salt and freshly ground black pepper

First make the filling. Mix the potato, minced beef, onion and garlic together in a large bowl. Add the melted butter, mustard seeds, turmeric and coriander, stirring to mix well. Season generously with salt and black pepper. Set aside whilst you prepare the pastry.

Preheat the oven to 200°C/Gas 6.

Cut the block of pastry into 6 even-size pieces. Lightly dust the worktop with a little flour and roll out each piece to a squarish shape, about 4mm thick. Divide the filling evenly across the middle of each pastry square.

Lightly brush the pastry edges with a little water, then bring up the sides to meet on top of the filling. Crimp and roll the edges together to completely seal the filling inside (rustic is a good thing here), placing the prepared pasties on one or two baking trays as you go. Brush all over with a little beaten egg to glaze.

Bake in the oven for about 35–40 minutes until deep golden brown and puffed up. Eat, preferably whilst still on the warm side of room temperature.

Free-form pork and pickle pies

These little pork pies use a hot water crust pastry as a sturdy shell to support the filling. Hot water crust is possibly the easiest of all pastries to make, as there is no rubbing-in and trying to keep it cool as you roll. Make these the night before you picnic, store in the fridge and serve cold, just like a traditional pork pie (except these ones have their pickle inside rather than on the edge of your plate, making them very handy for on-the-move eating).

MAKES 4 GENEROUS INDIVIDUAL PIES

For the hot water crust pastry
300g plain flour
1 tsp fine sea salt
1 egg
110ml cold water
60g butter, diced
60g lard, diced

For the filling
500g minced pork
6 rashers smoked streaky bacon, finely chopped
1 tsp dried mixed herbs
½ nutmeg, freshly grated
4 generous tsp chutney or pickle (of your choice)
Sea salt and freshly ground black pepper
Sea salt flakes, for sprinkling

To make the pastry, mix the flour and salt in a mixing bowl, make a well in the centre, then crack in the egg and flick a little flour over to cover it completely. Put the water, butter and lard into a pan and set over a medium heat. Stir as the fats melt and as soon as the liquid comes to the boil, tip into the mixing bowl, stirring well to form a soft ball. Tip on to the worktop and knead briefly, then cut into 4 even-size pieces (to help it cool quicker). Wrap in cling film, then chill in the fridge for around 30 minutes to firm up.

Meanwhile, make the filling. In a bowl, mix together the minced pork, bacon, herbs and nutmeg and season generously with salt and black pepper. Tip on to the worktop and divide into 4 even-size balls. Flatten each ball into a 1cm-thick disc, spoon some chutney into the centre of each, then bring up the sides to enclose the chutney completely. Set aside whilst you shape the pastry.

Preheat the oven to 180°C/Gas 4.

Cut about a third off each ball of pastry (this smaller piece will be the lid). For each pie, using your hands, flatten the larger piece to a 5mm-thick disc, then set a ball of filling in the middle. Shape the smaller piece of pastry to a 5mm-thick disc and drape over the top of the filling to create a lid. Bring the sides of the bottom pastry disc up to meet the lid, then crimp and press together to seal the filling inside completely. Repeat with the rest of the pastry and filling to make 4 pies. Use a skewer to pierce a generous hole in the top of each pie to let the steam out, then sprinkle over a few sea salt flakes and a grind of black pepper.

Place on a baking sheet and bake in the oven for about an hour until the pastry is crisp and golden. Leave to cool completely before wrapping and packing for your picnic.

Stilton, walnut and tarragon muffins

Muffins are a breeze to make, the beauty being that they need minimal mixing to make them light and fluffy, so they are about as hands-off as baking gets. These are great eaten on their own, preferably on the same day you bake them, or try them with a spoonful of the Peppered Onion Relish on page 36.

MAKES 6 BIG MUFFINS

Olive oil, for brushing
100g walnut pieces
175g Stilton, crumbled
150g self-raising flour, plus extra for dusting
½ tsp bicarbonate of soda

Small bunch of tarragon, leaves picked and chopped (about 2 tbsp)
2 eggs
200g plain yogurt
Sea salt and freshly ground black pepper

Preheat the oven to 200°C/Gas 6. Brush a 6-hole muffin tin (holes and tops too) with oil, then shake in some flour and tap around until the holes and around the tops are lightly coated, tapping out the excess.

Grind the walnuts in a food processor until they resemble crumbs, or crush them in a food bag with a rolling pin or using a large pestle and mortar. Tip into a mixing bowl, add the Stilton, flour, bicarbonate of soda and tarragon, season well with salt and black pepper, and mix well.

In another bowl, whisk together the eggs and yogurt, then pour into the dry ingredients and mix briefly until just combined. Lumps, and even little bits of dry flour, are just fine. Using two dessertspoons, fill the holes of the prepared tin. You can pile the mixture pretty high. These muffins will rise and spread a little out of the holes (which is why you have greased and floured the tops of the holes too, so they don't stick).

Bake in the oven for 20 minutes until golden brown. Leave to cool in the tin for a few minutes, then ease them out with a blunt knife on to a cooling rack. Cool completely.

Or how about a different flavour...?

- If you don't like Stilton, replace it with grated Cheddar, Gruyère or crumbled feta.

- You can also change the herbs – basil, parsley or thyme all work well.

- Try using different nuts – ground pecans are delicious, as are hazelnuts.

- Add a couple of tablespoons of chopped black olives, capers or sun-dried tomatoes.

- Stir through a little snipped-up cooked bacon, chopped salami or chorizo.

other savoury treats

Muffin tin frittatas with peas, ham and mozzarella

Mini frittatas are a brilliant way to use up bits and bobs from the fridge. Ring the changes any way you please, swapping the mozzarella for another cheese, or try using lightly cooked asparagus or green beans, or even a few slices of cold potato.

MAKES 6 MINI FRITTATAS

Butter or olive oil, for greasing
Couple of slices of ham, chopped
Handful of frozen peas (no need to defrost)
1 x 125g ball mozzarella, torn into little pieces

Small handful of basil leaves, chopped
5 eggs
A pinch of dried chilli flakes (optional)
Sea salt and freshly ground black pepper

Preheat the oven to 200°C/Gas 6. Grease a 6-hole muffin tin with butter or oil.

Divide the ham, peas, mozzarella and basil between the muffin tin holes.

In a jug, lightly whisk the eggs, then season with the chilli flakes, if using, and a little salt and black pepper. Pour slowly into the holes, letting the egg mixture settle to the bottom before adding more. The holes will be quite full.

Bake in the oven for 15 minutes until just set and light golden on top. Remove from the oven, leave to cool in the tin and serve at room temperature.

Southern-fried chicken bites

My son's favourite way with chicken, he'd eat these day and night if I indulged him. I have to be honest and say these are best eaten before they have been refrigerated. So I marinate them overnight, then roll in flour and quickly fry on the day I want to eat them.

SERVES ABOUT 4

600g skinless, boneless chicken thigh fillets,
   each cut into 4 pieces
3 tbsp plain yogurt
1 tsp fennel seeds, ground

½ tsp smoked paprika
Plain flour, for coating
Vegetable oil, for deep-frying
Sea salt and freshly ground black pepper

Start the night before you want to eat. Put the chicken into a bowl, stir in the yogurt, fennel and smoked paprika and season with salt and black pepper. Cover and refrigerate overnight (or for a minimum of 3 hours).

When you are ready to cook, put a good few tablespoons of flour into a bowl, then roll the marinated chicken, piece by piece, in the flour until it's well coated, transferring the coated pieces to a plate as you go.

Heat some oil in an electric deep-fat fryer or in a large, deep saucepan to 180°C (or until a small cube of bread sizzles and browns in less than 60 seconds), then deep-fry the chicken in batches for about 4–5 minutes until cooked, crisp and deep golden. Drain on kitchen paper. Serve whilst warm or within a couple of hours of cooking.

Thai-style Scotch eggs

Scotch eggs are quintessential picnic fare, principally because they travel so well and follow the golden picnic rule of tasting as nice, if not better, cold rather than hot. I like to eat these with sweet chilli sauce or with the Smoked Chilli Jelly on page 36.

MAKES 4 SCOTCH EGGS

5 eggs
500g minced pork
3 spring onions, finely chopped
2 cloves garlic, crushed
4 kaffir lime leaves, finely chopped (frozen taste better than dried)
1 stem lemongrass, tough outer part removed and inner part finely chopped

1–2 bird's eye chillies, finely chopped
Small bunch of coriander, chopped
1 tbsp fish sauce
1 tsp caster or granulated sugar
80g panko breadcrumbs
Vegetable oil, for deep-frying
Sea salt and freshly ground black pepper

Add 4 of the eggs to a pan of cold water and bring to the boil, then reduce to a simmer and cook for 5 minutes. Remove from the heat and run under cold water until cool. Peel, rinse and set aside.

Put the minced pork into a mixing bowl and add the spring onions, garlic, lime leaves, lemongrass, chillies, coriander, fish sauce and sugar and season to taste with salt and black pepper. Mix together thoroughly and set aside for 30 minutes or so for the flavours to infuse (or leave overnight in the fridge, along with the cooked eggs, if you prefer).

Lightly beat the remaining egg in a small bowl. Add the breadcrumbs to another bowl. Divide the minced pork mixture into 4 equal balls and flatten each one to about 1cm thickness. Place an egg in the centre of each. Fold the pork mixture up and around each egg, enclosing it completely and pressing any cracks together. Roll each one in the beaten egg, then in the breadcrumbs until coated.

Heat some oil in an electric deep-fat fryer or in a large, deep saucepan to 180°C (or until a small cube of bread sizzles and browns in less than 60 seconds), then deep-fry the coated eggs for 7–8 minutes until crisp and deep golden. Drain on kitchen paper and cool before serving.

Take your Scotch eggs around the world in flavours...

Use the same recipe and quantities of eggs, pork, onion, garlic and breadcrumbs given above and flavour the minced pork mixture with...

- **Caribbean** – add 2–3cm piece fresh ginger, finely grated, 1 teaspoon ground allspice, 1 teaspoon dried thyme, 1 Scotch bonnet chilli, deseeded and finely chopped, and 1 teaspoon soft brown sugar.

- **Moorish** – add 1 teaspoon *each* cumin, caraway and coriander seeds, all roughly ground, 1 teaspoon smoked paprika and a small bunch of flat-leaf parsley, chopped.

- **Indian** – stir through 1 tablespoon of your favourite curry powder, along with a small bunch of coriander, chopped.

what's for pudding?

Every picnic has to have a sweet course, but some things are going to work better than others. Sturdy cookies, brownies and muffins travel well and are easier to eat than cakes with gloopy icing or a cream-based filling. And unless you can keep them cold in a cool box, sweets like fudge, liquorice or even penny chews are going to fare much better than meltable chocolate bars.

For something a bit more healthy and refreshing, fruit almost always tastes better at room temperature, so can be a great picnic choice. Soft fruit, such as strawberries, raspberries and the like, are susceptible to squashing though, so I'd plump for something more protected. A whole melon is brilliant, providing you remember to pack a sharp knife to get into it. Kiwi fruit, cut in half and eaten with a spoon just as you would a boiled egg, are fun to eat. Or you can't beat a perfectly ripe bunch of grapes or some fresh juicy cherries for simplicity.

But if you fancy something a bit more substantial, here are a few delicious baked treats that pack up easily and travel well. These treats all keep well for around 5 days in an airtight tin or wrapped in foil.

Lemon and almond olive oil cookies

I made these cookies for a dairy-free friend of my son's and although it may sound a little strange, baking with olive oil is traditional in many countries around the Mediterranean. These are the easiest of cookies to make.

MAKES ABOUT 18 COOKIES

100g caster sugar
100g ground almonds
100g self-raising flour

100ml olive oil
1 egg
Finely grated zest of 2 large lemons

Preheat the oven to 200°C/Gas 6. Lightly grease 2 baking sheets.

Simply add all the ingredients to a food processor and whizz together until you have a soft, sticky dough (or mix by hand in a bowl with a wooden spoon).

Use your hands to roll the mixture into walnut-sized balls, then place them on the prepared baking sheets with plenty of space in-between. Using a dessertspoon, press each one out flat, to a thickness of around 1cm.

Bake in the oven for 10–12 minutes until pale golden. Transfer to a cooling rack using a palette knife and cool completely before storing in an airtight tin.

Flavour your cookies another way...

■ Add a handful of chocolate chips – milk, white or dark, as you wish.

■ Add a teaspoon *each* of vanilla extract and ground mixed spice for sweetly spiced cookies.

■ Add a couple of teaspoons of caraway seeds for an interesting taste.

Apple and blackberry crumble bars

These are like the best-ever apple and blackberry crumble in a cuttable, transportable bar. What's not to love? At their butteriest, crumbly best these can be a touch on the delicate side, so I tend to take the whole lot (already cut up) in the tin to protect them.

As well as being delicious, they freeze brilliantly when assembled but left uncooked. Simply freeze in the tin until solid, then remove from the tin using the baking paper to help lift the frozen block out. Wrap well and put back in to the freezer for up to 3 months. When you are ready to cook the crumble bars, slide the block back into the original tin and let it defrost, before baking as below.

MAKES ABOUT 15 BARS

2 medium cooking apples (about 550–600g whole/unprepared weight), peeled, cored and diced
150g fresh or frozen blackberries
2–3 tbsp granulated sugar, or to taste
100ml cold water

200g butter, softened, plus extra for greasing
200g soft light brown sugar
200g self-raising flour
1 tsp bicarbonate of soda
150g porridge oats

Preheat the oven to 200°C/Gas 6. Grease and line a 30 x 20 x 2cm baking tin with non-stick baking paper, leaving a couple of 'tails' to help lift it out.

Put the apples, blackberries, granulated sugar and water into a medium saucepan. Cover and simmer gently until soft, about 8–10 minutes. Remove from the heat and set aside.

Whizz together the butter and brown sugar in a food processor until creamed. Add the flour and bicarbonate of soda and pulse until combined (the mixture will be quite crumbly). Add the oats and pulse again to mix.

Tip about two-thirds of the crumble mixture into the prepared tin and press down well using the back of a spoon, covering the base completely. Spread the fruit mixture evenly over the top, then sprinkle over the remaining crumble mixture to cover the fruit completely.

Bake in the oven for 25 minutes until the top is crisp and golden. Leave to cool completely in the tin before cutting into bars.

And another thing...

- You can swap the blackberries for blackcurrants.

- Or replace the apples and blackberries with about the same weight of rhubarb. Simmer the fruit with 3–4 finely chopped pieces of crystallized ginger.

- Try substituting the cooked fruit with a jar (340g-ish) of your favourite jam.

Cappuccino blondies with walnuts and white chocolate

Coffee and walnut is my all-time fave cake flavour and a secret healthy ingredient in this version (it's actually a tin of cannellini beans, but ssshhhh, no one will ever tell!) means you can bake these blondies (like brownies but with white chocolate) without extra butter.

Whilst I don't really like the name 'traybake' (it seems just a touch too 'mumsy' for my liking), cakes cooked in a slab like this one are eminently practical for picnics as they cut and wrap neatly. You can even transport the lot in its tin, ready-cut, for extra sturdiness. (See photo on page 7.)

MAKES 12 SQUARES

Vegetable oil, for greasing
1 x 400g tin cannellini beans, drained and rinsed
3 eggs
125g caster sugar
300g white chocolate, finely chopped
125g walnuts, roughly chopped

75g plain flour
2 tbsp very strong (espresso strength) brewed coffee, cooled
2 tsp vanilla extract
2 tsp baking powder
½ tsp bicarbonate of soda

Preheat the oven to 200°C/Gas 6. Grease a 25cm square tin with oil and line with non-stick baking paper.

Tip the beans into a large mixing bowl, break in the eggs and add the sugar, then use a stick blender to purée them together to get a really smooth paste. This is what makes the beans 'disappear' so it's worth working at the mixture a little to get it smooth. Set aside.

Melt about two-thirds of the white chocolate in a heatproof bowl set over a pan of barely simmering water (reserve the remaining chocolate). Scrape the melted chocolate into the puréed bean mixture, along with the rest of the ingredients (except the reserved chocolate). Use a metal spoon to fold everything together into a smooth batter, then pour evenly into the prepared tin. Sprinkle over the rest of the white chocolate.

Bake in the oven for about 25 minutes until the blondie mixture is golden and starting to come away from the sides of the tin. A little bit of 'squidge' to the centre is just fine. Leave to cool completely in the tin before cutting into 12 squares.

Or try this...

- **Chocolate, orange and hazelnut brownies** – if coffee is not your thing, make a traditional brownie version by replacing the white chocolate with dark. Omit the coffee (replace it with milk) and instead add the finely grated zest of a large orange. Replace the walnuts with the same weight of roughly chopped hazelnuts.

some pickles to jazz up your picnic

Whilst a relish or sauce of some kind is often essential for a picnic, the most usual suspect, mayonnaise, isn't really the best traveller, unless you keep it cold with ice blocks. Hence, I prefer to take pickles on picnics, so here are a few of my favourites, which incidentally are all great for barbecue food as well.

Sterilizing the jars is the most important part of making pickles. A squeaky clean jar will mean whatever is inside will keep for much longer, so you can make a big batch safe in the knowledge it will last for ages, at least 6 months to a year. It's a very straightforward process, simply wash the jars and lids in warm soapy water, then rinse and shake off the excess water. Spread out on a baking tray and shove in a cool oven (around 110°C/Gas ¼) for about 30 minutes until completely dry.

All these recipes are best made a month or so before eating to allow the flavours to mature; they will keep for at least 6 months in a cool, dry cupboard, so they are just the sort of thing to make on a rainy day ready for when the sun comes out.

Fiery carrot pickle

This Indian-style pickle goes very well with the Bombay Spiced Beef and Potato Pasties on page 21, but try it also with your favourite cheese.

MAKES 4 STANDARD-SIZE (450G) JARS

300ml malt vinegar
300g granulated sugar
2 heaped tsp *each* dried chilli flakes and
   cumin seeds
2 heaped tsp coriander seeds,
   roughly ground

1 tsp ground turmeric
1 tsp sea salt
1.3kg carrots, peeled and grated
Small bunch of coriander, chopped

Add the vinegar, sugar, spices and salt to a large saucepan, then bring to a steady simmer, stirring until the sugar has dissolved. Add the carrots, stirring well, then cover and simmer for 10 minutes. Stir through the chopped coriander.

Remove from the heat, then pack into hot, sterilized jars. Cover and seal, then cool completely before storing.

Peppered onion relish

Caramelized onion relish is a true classic and tastes great with so many things, from cheeses and cold meats to pork pies and burgers. This version has crushed black peppercorns for a hit of heat, but leave them out if you prefer.

MAKES 4 STANDARD-SIZE (450G) JARS

1.5kg onions (5 large ones), thinly sliced
1kg granulated sugar
500ml sherry vinegar

4 tsp black peppercorns, crushed
1 tsp sea salt

Bung everything in a large saucepan and set over a medium heat. Bring to the boil, stirring from time to time, then turn down the heat to a steady simmer and cook for about an hour until the onions have turned a deep golden brown and are surrounded by a thick syrupy liquid.

Remove from the heat and leave to cool just a little before spooning into hot, sterilized jars. Cover and seal, then cool completely before storing.

Smoked chilli jelly

Hot, sweet and smoky, I love this with cold meats, or try it with the Thai-style Scotch Eggs on page 28.

MAKES 4 STANDARD-SIZE (450G) JARS

1 litre clear apple juice
1kg preserving sugar
  (this contains pectin to help the jelly set)

80g hot green or red chillies
  (bird's eye or finger ones are ideal), finely
  sliced into rounds (seeds and all)
1 tsp smoked paprika
1 tsp sea salt

Put a few saucers in the freezer to chill for testing the set as you cook. Add all the ingredients to a large saucepan and set over a medium heat, stirring from time to time, until the sugar has dissolved. Turn up the heat and boil rapidly for around 10–15 minutes, stirring occasionally.

After 10 minutes, begin testing for set by taking a chilled saucer and dribbling ½ teaspoon of the jelly mixture on to it. When it's cool, the jelly should wrinkle a little when you push it with your finger. Continue boiling and retesting until it does.

Remove from the heat and leave for 30 minutes before stirring to mix the chillies evenly, then pour into hot, sterilized jars. Cover and seal, then cool completely before storing.

Spiced cucumber slices

These delicately spiced cucumber slices add a nice little crunch to a sandwich, or try them with cold poached salmon.

MAKES 4 STANDARD-SIZE (450G) JARS

250ml white wine vinegar
250g granulated sugar
1 tbsp coriander seeds, roughly crushed
1 tsp *each* white peppercorns and allspice
   berries, roughly crushed

1 tsp ground turmeric
1 tsp sea salt
2 onions, thinly sliced
2 cucumbers, thinly sliced

Add the vinegar, sugar, spices and salt to a large saucepan, then bring slowly to a simmer, stirring until the sugar has dissolved. Add the onions, cover and simmer for 5 minutes. Stir in the cucumber slices and simmer, uncovered, for another 5 minutes.

Remove from the heat, then pack, liquid and all, into hot, sterilized jars. Cover and seal, then cool completely before storing.

And if you haven't got time for pickling...

Home-made pesto

Pesto is a complete doddle to make and tastes infinitely nicer than the shop-bought jarred stuff. It also travels well and jazzes up innumerable things. I love it with cheese or cold meats, or try it stirred through a simple pasta salad with tinned tuna. This pesto will keep for up to 3 days in the fridge. A layer of cling film pressed snugly on to the surface will stop it discolouring.

MAKES A DESSERT BOWLFUL

50g pine nuts
Large bunch of basil (about 100g), leaves
   and thinner stalks roughly torn
1 clove garlic, chopped

25g freshly grated Parmesan cheese
3 tbsp olive oil
Lemon juice, sea salt and freshly ground
   black pepper, to taste

Toast the pine nuts in a dry pan over a medium heat until they are golden and smell deliciously nutty. Tip them into a food processor and pulse until ground.

Add the basil, garlic, Parmesan and oil and pulse to a purée, adding just enough cold water to help it along. Season to taste with lemon juice, salt and black pepper.

Scrape into a bowl and chill in the fridge until needed.

three summery cordials

I'm a bit of a lightweight when it comes to alcohol in the daytime, so I pretty much always plump for soft drinks on a picnic, saving wine for when the sun is over the yardarm. But if you are made of sterner stuff than me, then I suggest you pack sturdy little glass tumblers. Wine in plastic glasses misses the point. And if it's white or rosé, be sure to have a way of keeping it cold because lukewarm wine that should be chilled is a non-starter.

Here are three summery cordial recipes that would be my choice on a picnic. Pack a bottle of cordial, along with a semi-frozen bottle of still water (which will also keep your food cool) or a well-chilled bottle of fizzy water, and then dilute to taste at your destination.

Elderflower cordial

A great cordial to make in May with young flower buds. This cordial keeps really well, for at least 2 months in the fridge in sterilized bottles (see page 34 for tips on sterilizing).

MAKES ABOUT 2 LITRES CORDIAL

2kg granulated sugar

1.5 litres cold water

20 fresh just-opened heads of elderflowers

3 lemons, cut into 5mm slices

60g citric acid (available from brewing shops or online)

Add the sugar and water to a large saucepan and set over a medium heat, stirring until the sugar has dissolved, then bring to the boil. Remove from the heat.

Wash the elderflower heads by dipping them quickly into a washing-up bowlful of cold water, shaking dry as you go, then drop them into the hot syrup. Add the lemon slices to the hot syrup, then add the citric acid and stir well.

Cover loosely with a clean tea towel and leave to infuse at room temperature for 24 hours, stirring a few times.

Strain through a muslin-lined sieve into a jug (in batches if necessary) before pouring into sterilized bottles, then seal and store in the fridge.

Serve diluted to taste with chilled still or fizzy water.

Raspberry cordial

The essence of raspberry in a glass, this cordial is great for when fresh raspberries are cheap and plentiful, but also when they are out of season, made using frozen fruit for a delicious reminder of summer days. It keeps for up to a week in the fridge, but also freezes brilliantly in ice-cube trays (single portions) or small plastic boxes for up to 3 months.

MAKES ABOUT 1 LITRE CORDIAL

600g fresh raspberries

300g granulated sugar

Juice of 1 lemon

1 litre cold water

Add the raspberries to a large saucepan, along with the sugar and lemon juice, then top up with the water. Bring slowly to the boil, stirring until the sugar has dissolved, then cover and simmer until the raspberries have collapsed, about 6–8 minutes. Remove from the heat and leave to cool completely.

Strain through a sieve into a large jug, pressing well to get as much juice out as possible. Cover and chill in the fridge until required.

Serve diluted to taste with chilled still or fizzy water.

Old-fashioned lemon and limeade

One sip of this citrus-burst of a drink will take you straight back to childhood summers. Like the Raspberry Cordial (see above), it keeps for up to a week in the fridge, but you can also freeze it in small containers for up to 3 months.

MAKES ABOUT 1.25 LITRES CORDIAL

3 large lemons

4 limes

300g granulated sugar

1 litre freshly boiled hot water

1 tsp citric acid

Finely grate the zest from the lemons and limes and add to a deep heatproof bowl. Squeeze in the juice from all the fruit (no need to worry about pips going in as it'll be strained later). Add the sugar, then pour in the freshly boiled hot water, stirring until the sugar has dissolved. Add the citric acid and stir well.

Cover loosely with a clean tea towel and leave to infuse at room temperature overnight or for up to 24 hours.

Strain through a sieve into a jug, then cover and chill in the fridge until required.

Serve diluted to taste with chilled still or fizzy water (about half cordial and half water is a good guide with this cordial).

BARBECUE
FEAST

Introduction

Often the first meal we turn to for al fresco entertaining, having friends over for a barbecue is enduringly the most popular way to eat outside. From about Easter onwards I grasp every opportunity possible to barbecue in the garden, and my favourite and most successful parties are often in the late spring, the atmosphere heady with the sense of a whole summer of fun stretching ahead.

Whilst cooking over fire no doubt makes food taste nicer – who can deny that a steak is not vastly improved by a gorgeously charred and crisp outside? – I think there is also much to be said for the edible memories that get dug up from the past when you barbecue. For me, cooking and eating in the garden, glass of wine close to hand, often reminds me of long ago holidays, conjuring up a sense of complete relaxation and freedom from the norm.

One of my very favourite barbecue moments was well over a decade ago whilst on honeymoon in Tobago, where we bought fresh tuna directly from a fisherman who'd dragged his boat on to the shore. We lit a disposable barbecue on the beach and cooked it there and then, accompanied by little more than a box of chips and a couple of beers from the beach bar, not to mention a few eager stray dogs. Simply heaven.

The very best barbecue food is all about bold flavours, colourful dishes that can easily be scaled up to feed a crowd, and food that doesn't try too hard but simply celebrates all we love about summer eating. As you have your kitchen and fridge close to hand, food can easily be prepared in advance, easing the pressure during the party. Most of the marinated meat and vegetable dishes in this chapter can be prepped ahead and kept covered in the fridge quite happily for 2–3 days. Close proximity to the fridge also means you can be more dairy heavy, and this is where I save my very favourite 'cream and fruit' pudding combos that I wouldn't dream of taking on a picnic or up a hillside.

This chapter includes lots of ideas for simple but stunning salads, and meat and fish marinated to perfection, plus a collection of lovely nibbles to keep people going while you fire up the coals.

THE BARBECUE – CHARCOAL OR GAS?

In terms of the necessary equipment, at its most simple all you need is to create a fire with some sort of grill above it to lay the food on. Barbecue purists (which I am most certainly not!) would say you need charcoal to get the best flavour from your cooking, and to some extent I would agree that real flames do give amazing results. But a gas-fired barbecue is a brilliantly convenient invention, and indeed what I have in my own garden. You just press a button, and within minutes you are cooking in a way that is no more time-consuming than lighting your hob or grill inside.

I have been known to barbecue something for dinner in the depths of winter just to get that amazing charred, caramelized flavour, and with the gas option I know for a fact that I barbecue more frequently than I would if I had to light a fire every time. That said, I do often light up my fire pit in the garden and use that as a barbecue when I feel a touch more adventurous (see page 76 for some fire pit cooking tips), but I like to know that both options are there.

Whichever way you choose to cook, a little preheating time is necessary. It takes 30–40 minutes of burning for charcoal to be ready to cook on, and about 10–15 minutes for a gas barbecue to get up to speed.

The right tools for the job

Apart from the barbecue itself, a few tools will make your life infinitely easier.

One thing that's really worth investing in is a barbecue grilling cage, basically a two-sided grill that is hinged at one end with some sort of handle for turning. These grilling cages are particularly good for cooking fish (either whole or fillets) or any other food that is a little on the delicate side or prone to sticking. I also find them useful for kebabs, so you can slide in several and turn them all over in one fell swoop. They have become really popular recently and should be very easy to find. I've even seen them in my local supermarket during the barbecue season.

The other barbecue tools I own are a set of long-handled metal implements, comprising tongs for turning sausages, a two-pronged fork for turning cuts of meat, and a spatula for flipping burgers or fish. Lastly, a stiff wire-bristled brush for scrubbing the grill after use is the most efficient way to clean your barbecue.

I generally like to keep gadgets to a minimum in my life, and any other fancy bits of barbecuing equipment are entirely optional to my mind, but I know some (men, I'm mostly looking at you!) will disagree, preferring to up the ante in the gear-stakes. That is entirely your choice.

HOW TO COOK ON A BARBECUE

Judging the temperature

Cooking on a barbecue is not a perfect science and you need a way to be able to judge temperature easily, and this is what I do. Simply hold your hand about 10–11cm over the heat (about the height of a tin of baked beans) and follow these rules for how long you can keep it there:

- 1–2 seconds – the heat is hot

- 3–4 seconds – the heat is medium-hot

- 5–6 seconds – the heat is medium

If you can hold your hand there for any longer it's probably a bit too cool to form the lovely caramelized crust you are after. With charcoal barbecues, bear in mind it is far easier to let the heat reduce than to increase the heat whilst you're cooking. So I would err on the side of caution and start by using more charcoal than you think you'll need.

WHEN IS IT COOKED?

Vegetables tend to just look 'done' when they are ready, but for meat and fish you need to be a little more certain to make sure your food is safe to eat. With a bit of practice you can use the 'prod test' with red meats, the principle being that meat becomes firmer as it becomes more cooked. Start by pressing the meat with a finger, then compare that feel to the feel of the base of the inside of your thumb as you touch your index finger and thumb together. If the meat is rare it will feel like when you touch your thumb and index finger together, basically soft and squidgy. As it becomes medium done, it feels the same as when you touch your thumb and middle finger together, then ring finger, and finally, well done meat should feel the same as when you touch your thumb and little finger together, much firmer to the touch. This method does take a bit of practice to be confident, so if you are in any doubt, check with a knife as well. With chicken, I would always recommend checking it in decent light with a knife to make sure there is no sign of pink before serving to your guests.

STICKING ISSUES

This can be quite a tough rule to follow, but don't be tempted to interfere too much with your food once you've laid it on the grill. Food will always stick initially but once it's been cooking for a bit a crust forms and you should be able to move it easily. So don't try and turn things over too much. Some food is naturally more prone to sticking – delicately textured food such as fish, or things that are naturally low in fat such as chicken breast – and this is where a barbecue grilling cage (see previous page) is a very useful bit of kit.

GETTING AHEAD OF THE GAME

Barbecuing is pure cooking theatre and people will naturally gather around you, watching you as you cook. Hopefully some may even offer to lend a hand (although don't be afraid to tell them to go away if you'd rather do it yourself!). To my mind this is all part of the fun of cooking outside, but it can be a little daunting if you're not used to cooking in front of a crowd, so it pays to get as organized as possible ahead of the game. I've tried to keep things simple by making the majority of the recipes in this chapter easy to prepare beforehand so that when your guests turn up hungry you can deliver them something delicious with the minimum fuss. My golden rule with all entertaining is to be disciplined and don't overstretch yourself. Do a few dishes and do them well rather than struggle to turn out a multitude of different things. I would rather eat one beautifully cooked, well-seasoned bit of meat or fish with a selection of simple interesting salads than an endless parade of sausages, burgers and kebabs.

eight easy ways to jazz up a jar of mayo

Home-made mayonnaise, thick and wobbly, occasionally has a place in my kitchen, but it is a treat usually reserved for (albeit rare) indulgent feasts of fresh crab or prawns. For more regular eating, I prefer the ready-made stuff, as it's a much lighter beast that goes with many more dishes, including salads, sarnies, cold meat and grilled fish.

To jazz up the flavour a bit, I often add a bit of this and that to suit what we're eating. Here are a few of my favourite flavoured mayos.

The amounts given are enough to season 3–4 generous tablespoons of mayo. To all of these I would also add a generous grind of black pepper.

- **Tarragon and chives** – add a tablespoon *each* of chopped tarragon leaves and chives. *Classic with simple barbecued chicken; also good with salmon steaks.*

- **Smoky chilli** – stir through ½–1 teaspoon smoked paprika and 1 finely chopped red chilli. *Lovely with home-made burgers or sausages.*

- **Sweet chilli and lime** – stir through 1 tablespoon sweet chilli sauce and the finely grated zest of 1 lime. Add a little lime juice for a sharper (and slightly runnier) dressing, or a little finely chopped red chilli for a hotter mayo. *Perfect with prawns or squid.*

- **Double mustard** – add a combo of smooth pungent English for heat and grainy wholegrain for texture. Mustard is a personal thing. I love the heat it gives so I add loads. Start with a heaped teaspoon of each, and increase to taste. *Good with pork chops.*

- **Lemon** – stir through the finely grated zest of 1 large lemon, plus a squeeze or two of juice to taste. *Perfect with simply grilled chicken or whole trout.*

- **Garlic and basil** – crush 1–2 cloves of garlic into a paste with a little sea salt, then mix in. Chop a small handful of basil leaves and stir through. *Great with a fat juicy steak or prawns.*

- **Tartare-ish with capers, gherkins and parsley** – mix together 1 tablespoon roughly chopped (drained) capers, a couple of finely chopped gherkins and a small handful of chopped flat-leaf parsley leaves, then stir through. *Good with all fish.*

- **Curry** – stir through 1 tablespoon of your favourite curry paste (paste gives a much better flavour than powder). *Great with all sorts of meaty kebabs, plus grilled vegetables.*

get-ahead DIY bruschetta

I don't really do 'starters' when I have friends over, preferring to take an informal approach to feeding people. But when you're barbecuing, things often take a little longer than you might plan for, so it's great to have plenty for everyone to nibble on to keep the hunger at bay.

My answer is to slice and toast a whole baguette (or two!) several hours ahead and then when people arrive, I pile them into a bowl and surround with various little dishes containing tasty bits of this and that. Add a bottle of good extra virgin olive oil and some crunchy sea salt flakes and let people tuck in.

Lots of almost instant bruschetta ideas...

- Whole tub of creamy ricotta, upended on to a saucer, scattered with a little finely chopped red chilli.

- Handful of lightly toasted pine nuts or chopped walnuts.

- Couple of balls of mozzarella, torn into bite-size pieces, scattered with plenty of roughly chopped basil.

- Generous plateful of serrano or Parma ham, or salami.

- Ready-made antipasti, such as chargrilled artichoke hearts, vinegary anchovies, sun-blush tomatoes or marinated red peppers.

- Tub of hummus (scoop it into a dish, scatter over some chopped parsley or a little paprika and drizzle over extra olive oil) or taramasalata (drizzle with olive oil and grate over some lemon zest).

- Dish of freshly shaved Parmesan (or even better, leave the whole wedge on a saucer with a vegetable peeler for people to do it themselves).

And a couple of things that take just a little more effort...

Red onion, black olive and sage salsa

This is great served with serrano ham or salami.

SERVES 4–6

1 red onion, very finely chopped	2–3 tbsp extra virgin olive oil
1 x 290g jar pitted Kalamata olives, drained and finely chopped	1–2 tbsp sherry vinegar
	Freshly ground black pepper, to taste
4 sage leaves, finely chopped	A pinch of caster sugar

Mix all the ingredients together in a bowl, adding the oil and vinegar to taste, and seasoning with plenty of black pepper and the caster sugar.

Smashed cannellini beans, capers and lemon

Lovely spread on toast whilst it's still warm.

SERVES 4–6

4 tbsp olive oil
1 large onion, finely chopped
2–3 sprigs of thyme or ½ tsp dried thyme
1 clove garlic, crushed
2 tbsp (drained) capers, roughly chopped

1 x 400g tin cannellini beans, drained
 and rinsed
Finely grated zest and juice of 1 lemon
Sea salt and freshly ground black pepper

Heat half of the oil in a frying pan and gently sweat the onion with the thyme over a very low heat until very soft and lightly caramelized, about 20–30 minutes. Remove the thyme stalks.

Add the garlic and capers and fry for a couple more minutes before tipping in the beans, along with the lemon zest and juice, mashing gently over a low heat until warm. Season with salt and black pepper, then drizzle with the remaining oil. Serve warm or at room temperature.

naan bread sticks with two tasty dips

I often make 'crisps' out of pitta bread – simply slice open, separate the 2 halves, sprinkle with dried chilli flakes, cumin seeds and salt to taste, drizzle with olive oil and bake until dry – then I decided to broaden out my easy-dipper repertoire by giving naan bread a similar treatment. So much nicer than bland, ready-made breadsticks, and a complete doddle to make.

Naan bread sticks

Preheat the oven to 180°C/Gas 4.

Slice as many naan breads as you want into 1cm strips (I allow about half a naan per person) and spread out over several baking trays. Drizzle over plenty of olive oil, then sprinkle over sea salt flakes and freshly ground black pepper. Add spices to taste if you like – cumin, fennel or caraway seeds are great, as are dried chilli flakes. Or buy flavoured naans (garlic and coriander ones are delicious) to keep it simple.

Bake in the oven for about 12 minutes, turning over halfway through, until crisp and dry. Leave to cool, then stick into glasses for serving. Made ahead of time, these keep for several weeks in an airtight tin.

And to serve with the bread sticks, make one (or both!) of these tasty dips...

Spiced cauliflower dip with Greek yogurt and roast garlic

SERVES 4–6

1 medium cauliflower, cut into florets
1 tbsp cumin seeds
1 tbsp coriander seeds
1 tsp dried chilli flakes, or to taste
3 tbsp olive oil
25g butter

6 cloves garlic, unpeeled
3 tbsp Greek yogurt
2 tbsp cold water
Squeeze of lemon juice, or to taste
Sea salt and freshly ground black pepper

Preheat the oven to 180°C/Gas 4.

Put the cauliflower florets into a roasting tin, then sprinkle over the cumin and coriander seeds, along with the chilli flakes. Season with a little salt and black pepper and drizzle over the oil. Dot with the butter and tuck in the garlic cloves. Cover loosely with foil and bake in the oven for about 1 hour, stirring once or twice, until the cauliflower is tender.

Remove from the oven and cool slightly, then tip into a blender or food processor, along with any juices, squeezing the garlic cloves out of their skins. Add the yogurt, along with the water, and blitz to a smooth, creamy purée. Sharpen to taste with the lemon juice and add a touch more seasoning, if necessary.

Scrape into a bowl and serve warm or at room temperature (this is best not served chilled).

Beetroot, goat's cheese and caraway dip

SERVES 4–6

1 x 250g packet ready-cooked beetroot
  (non-vinegary kind)
1 x 125g log creamy goat's cheese (rindless)
Dollop of crème fraîche

Small bunch of chives, snipped
1 tsp caraway seeds
1–2 tsp red wine vinegar
Sea salt and freshly ground black pepper

Put all the ingredients into a blender or food processor and blitz to a smooth and vividly pink purée. Adjust the seasoning to taste with the vinegar, salt and black pepper. Scoop into a bowl and serve at room temperature.

vegetables on the barbecue

Vegetarians can eat wonderfully well at a barbecue and these simple ideas are sure to go down a storm with everyone. Handily they can all be prepped ahead of time so will help you to get ahead of the game too. Once prepped, just keep them in the fridge overnight.

New potato, halloumi and sage kebabs

MAKES 6 KEBABS

400g new potatoes
Olive oil, for dressing
2 x 250g packs halloumi cheese,
  cut into cubes

Small handful of sage leaves
Sea salt and freshly ground black pepper

Put the potatoes in a pan, cover with cold water and add a shake of salt. Bring to the boil and cook until tender, about 15 minutes. Drain and cut in half, toss in a good slug of oil and season with salt and black pepper. Toss the halloumi separately in another good slug of oil, adding seasoning as you go.

Thread the potatoes and halloumi alternately on to 6 skewers, tucking the sage leaves in-between. Cook over a medium-hot barbecue for about 10 minutes, turning regularly, until evenly charred. Serve hot.

These kebabs are great served with one of the flavoured mayos on page 45.

Mini Mexican stuffed peppers

MAKES ABOUT 6 SKEWERS

2 tbsp olive oil, plus extra for drizzling
1 onion, finely chopped
2 cloves garlic, crushed
1 tsp cumin seeds
A pinch of dried chilli flakes

1 x 400g tin pinto beans, drained and rinsed
1 x 125g ball mozzarella, drained and finely
  diced
400g mini sweet peppers
Sea salt and freshly ground black pepper

Heat the oil in a frying pan and gently fry the onion until it is softening, about 10–15 minutes. Add the garlic, cumin seeds and chilli flakes and fry for a couple more minutes. Add the pinto beans and fry for a few more minutes, mashing up the beans with a wooden spoon. Season with salt and black pepper, remove from the heat and leave to cool. Stir the mozzarella through the cold bean mixture.

Cut the tops off the mini sweet peppers and use the handle of a teaspoon to scrape out the seeds. Fill each one with the bean mixture, popping the lids back on firmly. Carefully (they can be a bit tough) slide 2 or 3 filled peppers on to skewers, pushing them snugly up against each other.

Drizzle a little oil over the skewers and then cook over a medium-hot barbecue for around 10–15 minutes, turning regularly, until evenly charred. Serve hot.

Grilled courgettes and aubergines with chickpeas and tahini dressing

SERVES 4–6

100g tahini (sesame paste)
100ml cold water
Finely grated zest and juice of ½ lemon
1 clove garlic, crushed
A pinch of chilli powder (optional)
2–3 courgettes, cut lengthways into
   5mm-thick slices

2 aubergines, cut lengthways into
   5mm-thick slices
Olive oil, for brushing
1 x 400g tin chickpeas, drained and rinsed
Sea salt and freshly ground black pepper

Make a quick dressing by whisking together the tahini and water. Stir through the lemon zest and juice and garlic. Season with salt and black pepper, adding the chilli powder to taste, if you fancy. Set aside at room temperature, whilst you prepare and cook the veg.

Brush the courgette and aubergine slices on both sides with a little oil, then season with salt and black pepper. Cook over a medium-hot barbecue for a few minutes on each side, turning occasionally, until nicely coloured and cooked through.

Arrange on a serving platter (see previous page), scatter over the chickpeas, then drizzle on the dressing. Serve whilst the vegetables are still hot, or make a few hours ahead and rest at room temperature until you are ready to eat.

Garlic and thyme mushrooms in a foil bag

SERVES 4–6

500g mixed mushrooms, sliced or torn into
   bite-size pieces
2–3 cloves garlic, chopped

50g butter
Few sprigs of thyme
Sea salt and freshly ground black pepper

Tear off 2 generous sheets of foil and lay one on top of the other in a cross shape. Pile the mushrooms into the centre of the foil. Scatter with the garlic, dot with the butter, season well with salt and black pepper and then tuck in the thyme sprigs. Bring up the sides of the foil and scrunch together to make a sealed bag. Wrap the bag in a third sheet of foil to be completely certain it's sealed. Set aside at room temperature until you are ready to cook.

Place the foil bag over a medium-hot barbecue and cook for around 20 minutes, turning over a couple of times with tongs so the mushrooms cook evenly. Open up the bag and tip the mushrooms and all the delicious juices into a serving bowl (discard the thyme stalks).

Great served on their own, or use as a topping on either steak or beef or bean burgers.

Chargrilled asparagus and spring onions with Romesco sauce

In the Catalan region of northern Spain they adore eating calcots (a kind of giant succulent spring onion) charred over an open fire and eaten with a pungent pepper and garlic sauce called Romesco. Phenomenally popular, there are whole restaurants and even festivals dedicated to their consumption, but they're sadly almost impossible to source outside Spain. So here (see photo on page 51) is my British interpretation, using seasonal asparagus and fat spring onions.

The Romesco sauce will keep for a week or so in the fridge. It's best not served fridge-cold, so take it out a few hours before you want to eat.

SERVES 6

For the Romesco sauce
3 tbsp olive oil
2 large red peppers, deseeded and cut into 2cm pieces
50g whole blanched almonds
2 slices white bread, crusts removed
3 cloves garlic, crushed
½ tsp smoked paprika
1–2 tsp sherry vinegar
Sea salt and freshly ground black pepper

For the asparagus and spring onions
2 bundles of asparagus (about 250g each), woody ends trimmed
2 bunches of fat (sometimes called continental) spring onions, sliced in half lengthways
2 tbsp olive oil
Sea salt flakes, for sprinkling

To make the Romesco sauce, heat half of the oil in a heavy-based pan and fry the red peppers over a high heat for around 15–20 minutes, stirring regularly, until slightly charred in places.

Meanwhile, toast the almonds in a dry frying pan over a medium heat for a couple of minutes. Tip into a food processor and pulse until ground. Add the rest of the oil to the same pan and fry the bread slices on both sides until crisp. Leave to cool for a few minutes before crumbling into the food processor.

Add the cooked peppers (plus any cooking oil) to the food processor, along with the garlic and smoked paprika. Blitz, adding just enough cold water to make smooth. Season with a little vinegar, salt and black pepper, then set aside at room temperature until you are ready to serve.

Put the asparagus and spring onions into a large bowl and cover with cold water. Leave to soak for a few minutes (to remove any lurking grit), then drain and rinse.

When you are ready to eat, spread the asparagus and spring onions out on a baking tray and drizzle over the oil. Sprinkle generously with sea salt flakes and toss to mix well. Place over a hot barbecue for about 10 minutes, turning occasionally, until cooked and nicely charred in places. Pile on to a big serving plate and serve immediately with the Romesco sauce alongside to dip the veg in.

the best barbecue salads

The best salads are often the simplest, just a handful of top-notch ingredients treated with minimal fuss. Most, but not all, salads benefit from being served at room temperature. For example, anything tomato-based shouldn't be eaten chilled – you get ten times more flavour from a room temperature tomato than a chilly one. Ditto marinated Mediterranean-style veg like courgettes or aubergines. Lettuce, however, works best straight from the fridge and so does anything dairy-based that you top your salad with, such as cheese and creamy dressings.

Here are a few of my favourite easy salads for barbecue feasting.

Simple Greek salad

Mix together equal quantities of chunkily chopped **cucumber**, **tomatoes** and deseeded **green pepper**. Mix through a little thinly sliced **red onion** and a generous handful of pitted **Kalamata olives**. Sprinkle on a little **dried oregano**, then drizzle over **extra virgin olive oil** and a little **red wine vinegar**.

Set aside at room temperature for up to 1 hour before serving, or make ahead and keep in the fridge for up to 24 hours. Just before serving, give everything a quick mix before crumbling over some **feta cheese**.

Fresh figs and ricotta

Cut 6 **fresh figs**, warm from the sun (or at least warm from your kitchen windowsill!), into quarters, dot with spoonfuls of cold **ricotta**, scatter over chopped **basil leaves** and drizzle with plenty of **extra virgin olive oil**. Add a generous grind of black pepper and you've got a summery salad fit for a king.

Garlic and balsamic roast tomato salad

For jazzing up less-than-perfectly-ripe **tomatoes**, this salad is just the thing. Halve the tomatoes and lay cut-side up in a roasting tray. Slice up some cloves of **garlic** and poke a slice or two into each tomato half. Drizzle over a little **olive oil** and **balsamic vinegar** and season with salt and black pepper. Roast in a preheated oven at 180°C/Gas 4 for 40 minutes. Leave to cool to room temperature before serving.

Blue cheese and Little Gem

For each **Little Gem lettuce** (allow half a lettuce per person), blend together 50g **blue cheese** (Stilton is my favourite) with a heaped tablespoon of **soured cream** and a few snipped **chives**. A stick blender in a jug makes a smooth sauce, or mash the ingredients together with a fork for a more rustic version. Season with plenty of black pepper, then cover and chill in the fridge until you are ready to serve.

meat on the barbecue

Burgers – a barbecue essential

I think a good burger is probably the first thing people think of when you mention a barbecue and they are certainly a regular feature in our house. To my mind, there are two simple tricks to a good burger. Firstly, don't use mince that is too lean – I would always go for meat with a 20% fat content. Fat equals flavour and it also effectively bastes the meat as it cooks, keeping it juicy and delicious. Secondly, don't over handle the meat as you mix in the seasonings and shape your burgers. Too much squashing and squishing will compact the burger and make it dense and chewy rather than fall-apart tender.

Basic beef burger recipe

There are hundreds of recipes out there for beef burgers and this just happens to be mine. It's quick and simple, loved by grown-ups and kids alike and, best of all, it can be spruced up with all manner of toppings to elevate it to another league (see some tasty ideas opposite). The burgers will keep for up to 3 days in the fridge on a covered plate, or they can be frozen, well wrapped, for up to 3 months (defrost in the fridge overnight before cooking).

MAKES 6 GENEROUS MAN-APPETITE (i.e. ME) BURGERS
(MAKE THEM SMALLER IF YOU LIKE)

1 onion, very finely chopped or grated

2 tsp Marmite

1 tsp dried mixed herbs

1kg good-quality minced beef

Sea salt and freshly ground black pepper

Mix the onion, Marmite, herbs and salt and black pepper together in a mixing bowl to make a paste. Add the minced beef and mix the flavourings through lightly, then divide into 6 even-size balls. Flatten each one between the palms of your hands until about 1.5cm thick and 12cm in diameter. At this point, you can interleave the burgers with cling film or non-stick baking paper and refrigerate until you are ready to cook.

Grill the burgers on a medium-hot barbecue for about 3 minutes on each side or until cooked to your liking. Adopt a strict one-turn-only policy with your burgers – this not only allows a caramelized crust to develop which adds much in the flavour department, but it also minimizes the chances of the burgers falling apart. Serve with soft buns and toppings of your choice (see opposite).

A variation on your burger...

There is a multitude of ways to change this simple burger recipe, the easiest being to add flavour with spices – a generous pinch of any of the spice mixes on page 107 would be a great addition. Or swap the beef mince for another type of meat. Here are a few suggestions:

- With pork mince, Asian flavours work perfectly. Use the Thai-style Scotch egg recipe on page 28 as a base for delicious pork burgers – simply double up the quantities to make six generous burgers. Or, for a very British pork burger, mix the mince with chopped fresh sage, grated apple and a generous dollop of your favourite mustard.

- With lamb mince, try the Middle Eastern lamb and date burgers on page 88, or for classic lamb combos, mix the mince with plenty of freshly chopped mint or rosemary.

- Turkey mince is both affordable and nutritious, and makes a great base for a burger. To my mind, its mild flavour calls out for plenty of spicing to liven it up, and it also works well with Asian-style spicing. For a smoky turkey burger I would add a few rashers of finely chopped bacon or chorizo, along with a pinch of smoked paprika, as well as the finely chopped onion.

And something to put on your burger...

The joy of having a plain and simple burger is the fun you can have topping it. Here are a few of my favourite ideas...

- **Cheese** – blue, Cheddar, Brie and mozzarella all bring something special to the table; the main thing is to choose a 'melty' variety of cheese that'll ooze deliciously over the hot burger.

- **Crisp grilled bacon** – a classic burger combo, particularly if it's smoked.

- **Gherkins** – I know it is a bit 'golden arches', but there's a reason for adding them as the vinegary sharpness works wonders to balance the richness of the meat.

- **Chutney/pickle** – onion chutney, Indian spiced pickle, or even classic Branston are all fab.

- **Chilli sauce** – if you're a chilli fiend, you'll surely have your own favourite, but I particularly like anything made with fruity Scotch bonnet chillies.

- **Salad** – a bit of green crunch is good; peppery rocket or plain soft English lettuce are my favourites.

- **Avocado** – sliced thinly, adds a lovely creaminess.

- **Mayo** – always a winner (see page 45 for a few interesting flavours).

The perfect barbecued steak

Steak on a barbecue feels like a real treat and is great for spoiling yourself and your loved ones. Fillet steak is often thought to be the most prized cut (and therefore the most expensive), but to my mind it lacks in flavour and, being so lean, it can easily dry out. Steak that has a liberal marbling of fat throughout will be both juicy and tasty, and for that reason rib-eye is my go-to steak for a good balance between flavour and tenderness.

My preference is always to get a thick steak for sharing, and for this I visit my butcher who will cut it just as I like it. Ready-cut steaks from a supermarket tend to be on the thin side, which makes them rather too easy to overcook. With a thick steak you can get the outside really crisp and caramelized, which adds intensity to the flavour, whilst the inside stays as rare as you like.

The other cuts I love to barbecue are skirt steak and flank steak (which sometimes goes by the more glamorous name of 'bavette'). Both these cuts are economical and very tasty, but to stay tender they are best cooked very quickly over a high heat and served rather rare inside. To ensure it's extra tender, serve sliced across the grain.

Here is my favourite easy recipe for skirt or flank steak.

Black peppercorn and garlic bavette baps

SERVES 6

900g skirt or flank steak in one thickish
    piece (about 2cm thick or so, if possible)
2–3 cloves garlic, very thinly sliced
2 tbsp olive oil
2–3 tsp black peppercorns, crushed
Sea salt flakes, to taste

6 soft baps, cut in half
1 old-fashioned round English lettuce,
    leaves separated, washed and dried
Hot mustard or Double Mustard Mayo
    (see page 45), to taste

Lay the steak on a board and pierce all over using the tip of a cook's knife. Stuff slivers of garlic inside the slits, tucking it well inside the meat so it doesn't burn on the outside. Rub the steak all over with the oil, then sprinkle on the black pepper, rubbing it in on both sides. At this point your steak is ready to cook.

Get your barbecue really hot. Sear the steak over the barbecue for about 3 minutes on each side for a 2cm-thick steak, then remove and leave to rest on a board, loosely covered with foil, for about 10 minutes. This should give you a medium-rare steak; cook it for a little less if your steak is thinner, or more if it is thicker.

After resting, season with sea salt flakes, then thinly slice the steak across the grain and stuff into the baps with the lettuce leaves and a smear of hot mustard or Double Mustard Mayo.

Jerk chicken wings with coconut-bean rice and pineapple salsa

Jamaican jerk seasoning is a heady and addictive blend of herbs and spices and there are some really great ready-made spice mixes available. For this recipe, I grabbed a tin of my favourite brand to make it extra easy, but if you fancy having a go at mixing your own blend, try experimenting with ground allspice, dried thyme, finely chopped (deseeded) Scotch bonnet chillies and crushed garlic.

SERVES 4–6

1kg chicken wings
2 tbsp olive oil
2–3 tbsp jerk spice rub

For the rice
300g basmati rice
1 x 400ml tin coconut milk
200ml cold water
1 tbsp jerk spice rub
1 x 400g tin black-eye or black turtle beans, drained and rinsed
Sea salt and freshly ground black pepper

For the salsa
½ fresh pineapple, peeled, cored and finely diced
3 shallots, finely chopped
Handful of coriander leaves, roughly chopped
Finely grated zest and juice of 1 lime
2–3 red chillies, chopped
1–2 tsp caster sugar

Spread the chicken wings out over 1 or 2 baking trays and drizzle over the oil. Sprinkle with the jerk spice, then rub it all over the wings (use gloves if your skin is sensitive to chilli). Set aside for at least 1 hour in the fridge or, even better, overnight.

Begin the rice and salsa about 1 hour before you want to eat. Put the rice, coconut milk, water and jerk spice into a medium saucepan with a snug-fitting lid. Stir well and leave to soak for 30 minutes. Stir the beans through the rice and season with salt and black pepper. Set over a medium heat, bring to the boil, clamp on the lid tightly and boil for exactly 1 minute. Turn off the heat and do not remove the lid. Leave the rice to finish cooking undisturbed for 13 minutes. Lightly fluff up the rice with a fork, re-cover and set aside to keep warm whilst the chicken is cooking.

Make the salsa by combining all the ingredients in a bowl. Set aside at room temperature to allow the flavours to develop whilst you cook the chicken.

Cook the chicken wings over a medium-hot barbecue, turning regularly, for around 20 minutes. If they are colouring too much, move them to a slightly cooler part of the grill so they cook through to the centre without burning.

To serve, spoon the rice on to a platter and pile the chicken wings on top. Serve the salsa in a small bowl alongside for people to help themselves.

Butterflied lamb with garlic and rosemary

Lamb is perhaps the perfect red meat for the barbecue as it's liberally and evenly marbled with fat, so the meat effectively self-bastes as it grills. Perfect served crisp on the outside and pink in the middle, lamb is best cooked fairly quickly over a hot barbecue.

Butterfly a whole leg of **lamb** out flat and stuff slivers of **garlic** and **rosemary sprigs** into deep slits in the meat. Drizzle with **olive oil** and cook over a hot barbecue for around 15 minutes on each side for medium-rare. A 1.5kg leg (bone-in weight) will serve around 6 people. Your butcher can help with the butterflying, but if you want to give it a go it's pretty easy – all you are doing is cutting the bone out and flattening the meat. Use a small, sharp knife to scrape along the bone to ease it away from the meat. A bit rough and ready is just fine!

Spiced lamb and apricot kebabs

Influenced by the North African tradition of serving meat with fruit, these spicy kebabs are delicious served simply with buttery couscous and a green salad. Toasting the cumin and coriander seeds is not essential but it does really 'wake up' the flavours, so I would recommend it.

SERVES 6

800g boneless lamb leg steaks, diced into 3–4cm cubes	2 tbsp paprika
6 fresh apricots	1–2 tsp dried chilli flakes
Olive oil, for drizzling	1 tsp ground cinnamon
Sea salt flakes, for sprinkling	1 tsp ground ginger
Handful of chopped coriander	1 tsp soft light brown sugar
	2 cloves garlic, crushed
For the spice paste	Finely grated zest and juice of 1 lemon
1 tbsp *each* cumin and coriander seeds	3 tbsp olive oil
	Sea salt and freshly ground black pepper

First make the spice paste. Heat a small, dry frying pan, toast the cumin and coriander seeds together for a minute or so, then grind roughly using a pestle and mortar. Add everything else to the ground seeds, seasoning with salt and black pepper as you go, and mix to a paste.

Add the spice paste to the lamb and mix it thoroughly through the meat. Cover and leave in the fridge for a couple of hours, or overnight if possible.

When you are ready to cook, cut the apricots in half and remove the stones. Thread the lamb on to skewers, dividing it evenly and adding 2 apricot halves to each skewer amongst the meat, then drizzle over a little oil.

Cook over a hot barbecue for about 7–8 minutes, turning occasionally, by which time the lamb should be lovely and crisp on the outside and just pink in the middle. Arrange on a serving plate, sprinkle with a few sea salt flakes and scatter over the chopped coriander.

Satay-style pork ribs with spicy peanut sauce

I love ribs, I think they appeal to the latent cave woman in me, but they are a bit of a hands-on eating experience, so use pork leg steaks or loin chops if you prefer, allowing one per person. For extra flavour in the sauce, pour any leftover marinade in along with the water – just be sure to boil it well so it cooks.

SERVES 4

For the ribs
1.5kg meaty pork ribs (sometimes called 'king' ribs)
Finely grated zest and juice of 2 limes
5 tbsp soy sauce
2 tbsp vegetable oil
2 shallots or 1 banana shallot, finely chopped
4 cloves garlic, crushed
3–4cm piece fresh ginger, peeled and finely grated
1 tbsp black peppercorns, roughly crushed
1 tbsp caster sugar
2 tsp ground turmeric

For the spicy peanut sauce
1 tbsp vegetable oil
2 shallots or 1 banana shallot, finely chopped
2 cloves garlic, chopped
1 stalk lemongrass, trimmed and finely chopped
½–1 tsp dried chilli flakes
200g roasted salted peanuts
1 x 160ml tin coconut cream
250ml cold water
1 tbsp soy sauce
1 tbsp soft dark brown sugar

To prepare the ribs, spread them out on a large baking tray. In a small bowl, mix together the lime zest and juice, soy sauce, oil, shallots, garlic, ginger, black pepper, sugar and turmeric. Pour over the ribs and rub in really well using your hands. Leave to marinate for at least 1 hour or overnight in the fridge.

When you are ready to cook, grill the ribs on a medium-hot barbecue for about 20 minutes, turning regularly. If they start to catch a little, move them to a cooler area of the grill. Reserve any leftover marinade to boil in the peanut sauce if you want, but add it along with the water to be sure it gets a good boil to cook it. Once the ribs are cooked, remove to a plate, cover with foil and leave to rest whilst you finish the sauce.

Heat the oil in a saucepan and gently fry the shallots, garlic, lemongrass and chilli flakes until the shallot is softening, about 10 minutes. Whizz the peanuts in a food processor until ground (or seal them in a ziplock food bag and crush with a rolling pin).

Tip the ground peanuts into the pan, along with the coconut cream, water, soy sauce and sugar, plus any reserved marinade, if you like. Stir well and bring to the boil, then reduce the heat to a steady simmer and cook until reduced to a spoonable consistency, stirring every now and then, about 15–20 minutes.

Serve the barbecued ribs with the spicy peanut sauce alongside in a bowl.

fish on the barbecue

I love to barbecue fish and some of my most memorable outdoor meals have come from the sea. Oily fish works best as it's less likely to dry out and generally has a good, firm texture so it doesn't fall apart. Whole trout, sardines or mackerel and tuna steaks are all great, but here is perhaps my favourite way with salmon.

Indian-spiced salmon with minted yogurt dressing

SERVES 4–6

1 tbsp coriander seeds
1 tbsp cumin seeds
1–2 tsp dried chilli flakes
½ tsp black peppercorns
½ cinnamon stick (about 4cm), crumbled
Seeds of 4 green cardamom pods
5 cloves
½ tsp sea salt
2 tbsp vegetable oil
600g boneless salmon fillet (skin on)

For the minted yogurt dressing
6 tbsp plain yogurt
Handful of mint leaves, finely chopped
1 clove garlic, crushed
Juice of ½ lemon
Sea salt and freshly ground black pepper
Small handful of chopped coriander, to garnish (optional)
Lemon wedges, to serve (optional)

Blitz the spices coarsely in a spice mill, or use a pestle and mortar and a bit of elbow grease, then mix with the salt and oil.

Using a sharp knife, slash the skin of the fish deeply, but not all the way through, at 1cm intervals. Rub the spice paste all over the fish, being a little more generous on the skin side, rubbing it well into the cuts you have made (the spices will flavour the fish deep inside). Leave to marinate for 30 minutes, covered but out of the fridge.

Transfer the salmon to a barbecue grilling cage (see page 43) and cook, skin-side down first, over a medium-hot barbecue for around 10–12 minutes, turning over halfway through, until deep golden and crispy. Transfer to a serving plate (use a blunt knife to release the fish from the cage – the non-skin side may stick a bit). Cover with foil and leave to rest for 5 minutes to let the fish finish cooking gently.

For the dressing, mix the yogurt, mint, garlic and lemon together in a bowl and season with salt and black pepper. Drizzle a little dressing over the fish, then scatter over the coriander, if using. Serve the rest of the dressing on the side.

Kiwi-marinated squid with chermoula dressing

Marinating with kiwi is an antipodean thing, a tip picked up and handed on via my husband's travels to Australia many moons ago. The fruit contains an enzyme that tenderizes in a way that nothing else does and it's particularly effective with squid that can have a tendency to toughen up on cooking. The squid doesn't taste remotely of kiwi either, just in case you were wondering…!

I serve this barbecued squid with a chermoula dressing – chermoula is a pungent marinade from Tunisia and it works particularly well with seafood. It keeps well in the fridge for up to 3 days in a bowl covered with a layer of cling film pressed on to the surface.

SERVES 4

2 large squid, cleaned and left whole
2 kiwi fruit, peeled and roughly chopped
Olive oil, for drizzling
Sea salt flakes, for sprinkling, and
    freshly ground black pepper

For the chermoula dressing
5 tbsp olive oil

Finely grated zest and juice of 1 lemon
3 cloves garlic, chopped
1½ tbsp ground coriander
1 tsp smoked paprika
1 tsp ground cumin
1 tsp ground ginger
Small bunch of coriander, roughly chopped
Sea salt and freshly ground black pepper

First make the dressing. Put everything into a food processor, or use a stick blender in a jug, and process until smooth. Season with salt and black pepper. Leave at room temperature for an hour or so, if possible, to allow the flavours to mingle.

Prepare the squid. Remove the 'wings' from each squid and set aside. Slice each body down one side and open out so that it is flat, then cut in half, giving you a total of 4 body pieces (plus the 4 wings). Using a sharp knife, very lightly score all over the surface of the body pieces and wings in a diagonal pattern. Put the prepared squid into a large, flat dish, along with any tentacles.

Put the kiwi into a jug and purée with a stick blender, then pour on to the squid, spreading all over. Leave to marinate in the fridge for 30 minutes. Thread the squid (body pieces, wings and tentacles too) on to skewers (use a few skewers crossed over in a diamond shape to keep the squid pieces flat whilst they cook). Drizzle a little oil all over and sprinkle with a few sea salt flakes and a grind of black pepper.

Cook over a very hot barbecue for just a minute or two on each side, then serve immediately with the chermoula dressing to drizzle over.

puddings to finish the feast

Apricot and almond fool

Puddings made of a combo of fruit and cream tick all the right boxes in my book and none more so than fruit fools – such easy, impressive puddings that can be knocked up with minimal effort. This one, using a rich purée of dried apricots, was designed for a spring barbecue when the weather was lovely and warm but there was not a lot of decent ripe fruit to be found.

SERVES 6

350g dried apricots, roughly chopped
Finely grated zest and juice of 1 lemon
300ml cold water
100g whole blanched almonds
400ml double cream

1 tbsp icing sugar
2–3 tbsp amaretto (optional)
300g Greek yogurt
  (0%-fat is fine, if you prefer)
50g ratafia biscuits

Combine the apricots, lemon zest and juice and water in a saucepan. Bring to the boil, then reduce the heat, cover and simmer gently until very tender, about 15 minutes. Remove from the heat and use a stick blender to purée until smooth. Spread out in a shallow dish (this will cool it much quicker) and set aside until completely cold.

Meanwhile, preheat the oven to 200°C/Gas 6. Spread the almonds out on a baking tray and toast in the oven until golden brown, about 8–10 minutes. Do set a timer here as they burn really easily (I speak from bitter experience!). Leave to cool, then roughly chop.

Pour the cream into a large mixing bowl, sprinkle over the icing sugar and add the amaretto, if using (start with a couple of tablespoons, you can always add a little more to taste). Whip until thick and holding soft peaks. Taste, adding a splash more amaretto if you fancy, then fold in the yogurt thoroughly. Lightly fold through the cold apricot purée and most of the almonds, leaving it ripply, then scoop into a serving dish. Cover and chill in the fridge until needed (overnight is fine).

Just before serving, sprinkle over the rest of the chopped almonds and the ratafia biscuits, roughly crushing them in your hands as you go.

A couple of other favourite fools…

As the seasons change I alter the fruit I use – rhubarb, gooseberries, raspberries, blackcurrants and plums all get the fool treatment, using the same basic quantities of cream, icing sugar and yogurt. Here are my two other favourites:

- Simmer about 500g topped and tailed **gooseberries** with a splash of **elderflower cordial**, and sweeten to taste before cooling. This is great sprinkled with crumbled ginger biscuits.

- Stone and chop 650g **plums** and simmer with a pinch of **ground cinnamon**, and sweeten to taste before cooling. This works brilliantly with the crumbled ratafia biscuits.

White chocolate and blackcurrant tart with gingernut crumb base

I've never been 100 per cent certain about the merits of white chocolate – it always felt a little sweet and, dare I say it, one-dimensional. That was until I teamed it up with a vibrant blackcurrant compote in this tart. Quite a thing to look at, and a real explosion of tastes, this is a winner. There are a few cooling and chilling stages, but it can happily be made the day before and kept in the fridge overnight.

SERVES 6-ISH

200g gingernut biscuits
100g butter, melted, plus extra for greasing
400g white chocolate, broken into pieces
200ml double cream

½ tsp vanilla extract
250g blackcurrants (fresh or frozen)
1 tbsp cold water
2–3 tbsp granulated sugar

Lightly grease a 25cm loose-based flan tin.

Whizz the gingernuts in a food processor until they form fine crumbs. Stir through the melted butter, tip into the prepared tin and press down firmly with the back of a metal spoon, taking the mixture up the sides as well as over the base. Chill in the fridge for 30 minutes until firm.

For the filling, put 350g of the white chocolate, along with the cream and vanilla extract, into a heatproof bowl set over a pan of barely simmering water. Leave the chocolate to melt, stirring frequently, until you have a thick, shiny sauce. Pour over the chilled gingernut base, transfer to the fridge and leave to set firm, ideally overnight, but 3–4 hours at a push.

Meanwhile, put the blackcurrants, water and sugar into a small pan and simmer over a low heat until soft. Remove from the heat and cool completely. Once the filling has set, pour the cold blackcurrant compote over, spreading it to the edges.

Melt the remaining white chocolate in a small heatproof bowl as before. Using a teaspoon, drizzle the melted chocolate over the blackcurrant topping, then set aside at a cool room temperature until set. Release the tart from the tin and transfer to a serving plate. It will keep for a few days in the fridge, but I guarantee it won't be around that long.

Pimm's jelly with strawberries and minted cucumber cream

Who says jelly and cream is just for kids? This boozy version is inspired by a classic Pimm's cocktail and is very refreshing and summery. You need to start this recipe the night before you want to eat it as it needs plenty of time to set.

SERVES 6

8 sheets of leaf gelatine (about 16g)
400ml Pimm's No. 1
2 x 330ml cans clear lemonade
300g strawberries, hulled
½ large cucumber

1 x 170ml carton double cream
3 sprigs of mint, leaves picked and finely
  chopped
2 tbsp icing sugar

Add the gelatine leaves to a bowl of cold water, one at a time to prevent them clumping together, and leave to soak for 10 minutes.

Measure the Pimm's into a large jug and top up with the lemonade, then pour around 200ml into a small saucepan. Warm gently, but don't boil, then remove from the heat. Remove the gelatine leaves from the soaking water and squeeze out any excess liquid before dropping them into the pan, stirring well until completely melted. Pour back into the jug of Pimm's mixture and stir thoroughly, then pour the lot into a large serving bowl.

Cut half of the strawberries into quarters (reserve the rest for decoration), sliding them into the jelly as you go. Carefully transfer the bowl to the fridge and leave to set overnight.

Use a zester or small, sharp knife to peel long thin strips of peel from the cucumber and drop into a bowl of cold water. Pop in the fridge, where they will curl up into pretty spirals. Grate the cucumber into a small bowl, then stir through the cream and mint. Cover and leave to infuse in the fridge overnight.

The next day, tip the infused cream into a fine-meshed sieve placed over a mixing bowl, then use the back of a spoon to squeeze as much cream through as possible. Discard the cucumber and mint. Add the icing sugar to the cream and lightly whip to form very soft peaks. Spoon into a serving dish to serve alongside the jelly.

Decorate the jelly with the remaining strawberries, chopping or slicing them as you wish. Finally, remove the cucumber peel from the water and carefully pat dry, before sprinkling over the top.

And finally, a few speedy ideas for kids...

I can offer my kids as many delicious puddings as I can come up with but the simple fact is that they, and I'm sure other people's too, like the simple sweet things best. Basically, that means vanilla ice cream, so here are a few of their best ideas to top it with...

- Melted Mars bar sauce, a blast from my childhood – simply chop up a few Mars bars and melt them in a heatproof bowl set over a pan of barely simmering water. They will set back to a toffee-ish sauce when poured over cold ice cream.

- Give Toblerone the same melting treatment, or try Snickers bars for a nutty toffee explosion.

- Chopped nuts – brazils, pecans and walnuts are favourites in our house.

- Chopped or whole fruit, such as peaches, nectarines, strawberries or raspberries.

- White, dark or milk chocolate chips.

- Multi-coloured sugar sprinkles in the full rainbow spectrum.

BONFIRE
CELEBRATIONS

Introduction

Although a part of me will always mourn the end of summer, I absolutely love the autumn; I might even stick my neck on the line and say it is my favourite season. I think in part it stems back to childhood and the memories of running wild outside during the festivities of Halloween and Bonfire Night. That and the fact that my birthday is in the early autumn, plus both my kids are October-born babies, so it all adds up to a season of sheer celebration.

In my memory, these long-ago bonfire parties were full of the food of childhood fantasies – an all-you-can-eat buffet of things normally heavily rationed, like buttery crisp toffee apples, burgers dripping with fried onions and stuffed into squishy white buns (the usual wholesome brown thankfully nowhere to be seen), hot dogs drenched in ketchup, froths of pink candyfloss wound round and round sticks until they were bigger than our own heads, and oozing marshmallows toasted to the point of utter perfection.

Just as with open fires within the home, bonfires have a wonderful way of drawing people in and I relish cooking over a fire in the autumn (and even in winter) as a way of staying connected to the outside for more of the year. Sometimes, as a Friday night treat to celebrate the end of a long week at school, the kids and I light the fire pit in the backyard and they cook their own sausages on it, shoving them on to forks wired to long bamboo sticks. Mummy usually has a glass of wine, and we sit around the fire as the sun goes down, and even though it's just a few bangers for tea, it feels like both the most exciting and the most relaxing part of the week. I absolutely love it when I tuck the kids up in their beds afterwards and, as I kiss them goodnight, they smell gorgeously feral, the wonderful whiff of wood smoke and of memory-making small adventures.

This chapter is about getting both kids and grown-ups outside and creating a sense of space, adventure and freedom, even if it's only in your own garden. Here is a celebration of fabulous low-fuss food for cooking over an open fire, with recipes to warm body and soul, inspired by the nostalgic festivals of Halloween and Bonfire Night. It's also worth noting that many of the ideas and recipes in this chapter are equally well suited to camping trips, so don't feel constrained about taking them further afield.

GETTING AHEAD

Some of the recipes in this chapter are designed to be made, or at least started, in the comfort of your own kitchen. This simply makes life a bit easier for yourself and I'm all for that. The Pumpkin Soup with Chilli Beef Sprinkles (see page 80) was designed for quick reheating in an old pan over the fire after a bit of Halloween trick or treating, and both the Best-ever Spiced Chicken Kebabs (see page 88) and the Middle Eastern Lamb and Date Burgers (see page 88) can be made up to 24 hours ahead of time and stored in the fridge.

For the things that I cook directly over the fire (for example, the Rabbit, Bacon and Pearl Barley Stew on page 90, and the Cowboy Chilli with Cornbread Dumplings on page 92), I generally do the chopping of veg earlier in the day and store in food bags ready to cook over the fire later on. Then I just need to upend the bags into the pan to get going, thus minimizing the need to nip back into the kitchen for things I forgot.

HOW TO COOK OVER REAL FIRE

Cooking over fire is something of an art rather than a science and it's hard for me to give definitive and precise timings for these recipes (in the way that I would if I were writing a recipe for a hob or a conventional oven in your kitchen).

Every fire I light is different in terms of heat and intensity, and so too will every fire you make, so cooking in this way needs a certain level of adaptability and flexibility. Many factors will affect the heat your fire gives you for cooking, including how wet or dry your fuel is, the direction and strength of the wind, the rain that may be threatening to fall, or simply the level of humidity in the air. If you are cooking over fire you need to use your instinct, trust your judgement and get used to using your senses as you cook, principally nose and eyes, to test for readiness. For me, this is part of the joy of cooking outside; you are not simply following somebody else's formula for success but getting really connected to the cooking process. One thing I have learnt, and possibly the most valuable tip I can offer you, is always to expect it to take longer than you think. As all parents know there isn't much worse than the temper of a hungry child, and I'm not much better myself to be honest, so for this reason it's wise to have a hearty selection of snacks available to stave off hunger whilst the fire does its thing.

Regarding the cooking temperature of your fire, the hand-heat test in the Barbecue Feast chapter on page 43 is a good guide for open fires too.

FUEL MATTERS

I usually start a fire in one of two ways. Either with a firelighter and few little bits of kindling, or with a super handy (but quite pricey) bag of instant lighting charcoal. One match and, in theory, you are good to go. Either way, I follow the fire-starting process with plenty of lumpwood charcoal, which gives a pretty reliable and even cooking temperature. Then depending on where I am cooking, I may add extra wood foraged from the forest floor or driftwood gathered from the tideline. Sending the kids off to collect wood for burning is a splendid way to gainfully occupy them whilst you're busy getting organized. It's worth bearing in mind though that foraged wood can be damp and, hence, can lower the heat of your fire considerably, so I suggest adding it little by little rather than dumping on masses of sticks at once.

EQUIPMENT ESSENTIALS

It may sound obvious, but at its most minimal, all you need is somewhere to light a little fire. A cheap garden brazier is enough to provide much joyous warmth to huddle around as you toast a few marshmallows on an autumn evening. But my guess is that if you are reading this chapter you are ready to be a bit more adventurous, so below is a list of the bits of fire cooking kit that I would recommend investing in. All these things can be easily bought online, and there are plenty of specialist fire cooking websites out there where you can both shop and get advice.

Portable fire pit

I have a lightweight shallow circular bowl fire pit with four legs that fold ingeniously up underneath when not in use. The whole lot packs down and slides into a slim bag with handles, making it very easy to throw in the back of the car to take off camping or wherever I want to use it. The brilliant thing about it is that as it raises the fire off the ground, pretty much every campsite I've been to is happy for me to use it as they don't class it as a bonfire that would damage their land. It's not just useful for camping trips, this is what I often use in the garden as it's a relatively safe way to have a controlled open fire in a smallish space.

Campfire tripod with cooking grill

I have a sturdy cast-iron tripod that straddles the fire and on to it hangs a cooking grill that you can barbecue on. The grill is attached to the tripod with chains so you can raise or lower it to adjust the cooking temperature. There is also a central hook with a chain on to which you can hang an ever-useful Dutch oven (see below) or a kettle. I admit it's a heavy bit of kit, and certainly not one you can carry too far from your vehicle, but it's a brilliant bit of camp-cooking equipment that I find invaluable.

A Dutch oven

Another rather heavy cooking item that isn't designed to be carried too far, but one that I wouldn't be without, is my Dutch oven – a solid cast-iron cooking pot that either hangs above the fire from a tripod or gets buried in the embers. Visually it brings to mind a bubbling witch's cauldron and it certainly gets a lot of admiring attention. Not just handsome to look at, it's tremendously useful – as well as stewing and slow roasting, you can also use it for baking. With a little bit of practice, you can use it to make a great loaf of bread or even a cake by putting hot coals directly on to the heavy cast-iron lid, thus creating top heat to brown things. It does take a bit of getting used to to get the heat right, and like all fire-based cooking, success is somewhat down to a combination of suck-it-and-see and instinct. But when you get it right, the results are spectacular.

Fireproof pots and pans

I have some heavy-duty steel frying pans that I can either nestle directly into the embers of a fire, or more usually place on to the cooking grill above it. These frying pans are the cheapest ones in the cook shop, no fancy non-stick coating, no fancy plastic handles that would melt, and they are so solid I feel like they will last a lifetime. They benefit from 'seasoning' at home to get them fire-ready, a bit more non-stick and less likely to rust. Simply wash each pan well with warm soapy water, rinse and dry, then set over a medium-high heat. Pour in a little vegetable oil and spread it all over the inside of the pan with a scrunched-up bit of kitchen paper so it's completely coated. Bake on the oil until it's pretty much dry – this can take 10–15 minutes, and it gets a bit smoky so an extractor fan is useful (or even better, do it over the fire outside so there's no smoky kitchen to worry about). You may need to repeat this process again from time to time to keep the pans in tip-top condition.

I have two large 30cm frying pans, perfect for paellas, fry-ups and pancakes, plus a smaller 23cm one, perfect for frying eggs or even heating up a couple of tins of baked beans. I also have a big old saucepan with metal handles and a lid that goes on to the fire grill, in which I make popcorn or use for simmering or reheating soups and stews.

And finally, a box of tricks...

To make my life simple, I keep a big sturdy plastic box in my shed that is packed full of bits and bobs that I use regularly. So in it is a box each of firelighters and matches, as well as a selection of enamel mugs and plates, and a plastic tub of old cutlery. This is also where I keep my frying pans and a collection of nothing-special cooking utensils (a few wooden spoons and a couple of heatproof silicone spatulas, as well as some long-handled tongs for turning things over) I have gathered from cheap kitchenware shops. There is also a roll of foil and one of kitchen paper towels, plus a pack of non-scented baby wipes for hand-wiping. A few pairs of disposable latex gloves are very useful to have packed any time you are handling meat or fish to cut down on the need for hand washing. Nothing in this box is valuable or irreplaceable but it's all super handy, and having it there ultimately means I'm pretty much ready to cook outside whenever the mood takes me, and so I do it more often as it's far easier to get organized.

fast and fuss-free

Fancy dogs

One of the best birthday parties we ever had was a few years ago in the woods below our house. The kids invited a few friends each and their parents were welcome, as were canine family members. I borrowed a wheelbarrow and into it we piled a gas stove, a big saucepan and industrial quantities of hot dogs, not forgetting the biggest bottle of ketchup we could find and a bucketful of cold beer for the grownups. It was complete chaos, no games or organized fun to be found, just feral muddy kids, overexcited dogs and a whole lot of enthusiastic eating and drinking.

Obviously the hot dogs were exceedingly popular with the kids, but that the adults consumed them with so much gusto was perhaps surprising. They take just minutes to cook, making them super convenient, and now they are a regular fixture for our outside eating treats, both when we have a bonfire or when we are camping.

One hot dog in a roll never seems quite enough for me, the ratio of bread to sausage is tipped in the wrong direction, so I take one roll and put two hot dogs in it. Whilst my kids like them plain and simple with just a squiggle of ketchup across the top, I've taken to a bit of experimenting with different flavours, and below are a few ideas. I suggest you assemble a few different toppings and let people construct their own idea of hot dog heaven.

- **Mustard** – Americans would probably insist on the mild vivid yellow stuff, but I like a bit more oomph so favour Dijon or good old English mustard.

- **Onions** – fried long and slow until they form a soft caramelized golden mass (I do this at home, then pack into an old pan, ready for reheating on the stove or fire).

- **Chilli** – as a bit of a heat-fiend this is a favourite of mine, either as a garlicky chilli sauce, like sriracha, or a few slivers of fresh red chilli sprinkled on top.

- **Cheese** – Cheddar suits everyone and is my favourite, especially with a few fried onions and a bit of chilli sauce.

- **Hummus and roasted peppers** – a spoonful of hummus in the base of the roll, followed by the hot dogs, then topped with a few slivers of roasted red pepper from a jar.

- **Kimchi** – Korean fermented vegetables (predominantly cabbage and carrots) are a trendy pickle right now, taking the place of sauerkraut in adding a bit of zing.

- **Bacon** – two crisp rashers of smoked streaky bacon, one either side of the hot dog, adds a very pleasing salty crunch.

- **Avocado** – roughly chopped and squidged into the roll before the hot dog, then sprinkled with a little chopped coriander and/or fresh chilli.

- **Coleslaw** – a little bit of crunch can be a good thing and coleslaw (especially home-made) fits the bill perfectly. Try the Asian-style Slaw with Peanuts, Lime and Sesame Oil (see page 17).

Pumpkin soup with chilli beef sprinkles

A great one to serve after fireworks or after Halloween trick or treating, make this autumnal soup ahead and reheat on the hob or, even better, in an old pan over the fire when everyone is ready to be warmed up from the inside out! It keeps in the fridge for up to 3 days and also freezes well (minus the beef sprinkles, which are best made on the day of eating), so is a good one for batch-cooking. A word of warning – the flesh of carving pumpkins is very watery and often tasteless, so although it's tempting to use the leftovers, in this instance it's better to buy pumpkin that is specifically for eating purposes.

SERVES 4–6

For the soup
2 tbsp olive oil
2 onions, chopped
2 cloves garlic, crushed
1kg pumpkin flesh, peeled, deseeded and cut into 2cm cubes (or use any variety of squash)
1 litre vegetable or chicken stock
2 bay leaves
Sea salt and freshly ground black pepper

For the chilli beef sprinkles
2 tbsp olive oil
250g lean minced beef
2 cloves garlic, chopped
2 tsp cumin seeds
1 tsp smoked paprika
Hot chilli sauce, to taste
A little chopped coriander, to garnish

To make the soup, heat the oil in a large pan and gently fry the onions for around 15 minutes until turning golden. Add the garlic and pumpkin and fry for a further minute, then add the stock. Drop in the bay leaves and season well with salt and black pepper. Cover with a loose-fitting lid and simmer gently until the pumpkin is soft and collapsing, about 20 minutes.

Fish out the bay leaves, then purée the mixture until smooth, either with a stick blender in the pan, or by transferring to a blender. Taste to check the seasoning, then transfer to a suitable container, cool, cover and chill in the fridge until you are ready to serve.

For the chilli beef sprinkles, heat the oil in a frying pan and add the minced beef. Fry over a high heat, stirring and breaking up with a spoon to separate the meat into little strands. When the meat is cooked, crisp and caramelized, stir through the garlic, cumin seeds, paprika and chilli sauce and fry for a further minute. Remove from the heat and set aside until you are ready to serve (preferably out of the way; they are very tempting to nibble on!).

Reheat the soup until piping hot and serve with the chilli beef sprinkles scattered on top. Garnish with a little chopped coriander.

Fire-baked sweet potatoes with balsamic onions, blue cheese and walnuts

Sweet potatoes bake brilliantly in the embers of a fire and as a bonus they cook far quicker than regular potatoes. I find a punchy sweet and sour filling, like this onion and blue cheese combo, works best to counter the sweetness of the potatoes, or try one of the other easy ideas below.

SERVES 4

1 tbsp olive oil
25g butter
3 large onions, sliced
2 sprigs of rosemary, leaves picked and
  chopped
1 tbsp balsamic vinegar

A pinch of sugar
4 large (about 350g each) sweet potatoes
250g soft blue cheese, such as Gorgonzola
  or Roquefort, chopped
50g walnut pieces, roughly chopped
Sea salt and freshly ground black pepper

Start by cooking the onions – they keep well in the fridge and can be made up to 3 days in advance and then warmed through just before serving. Add the oil and butter to a frying pan set over a low heat. As the butter melts, add the onions and rosemary and fry gently for around 30 minutes, stirring from time to time, until starting to colour a little.

Add the balsamic vinegar and sugar and season with salt and black pepper. Increase the heat to medium and cook for a further 20 minutes or so, stirring occasionally, until caramelized. Remove from the heat and set aside until you are ready to eat.

Prick the potatoes all over with a fork and wrap each one in a double layer of foil, then pop into the glowing embers of the fire. Use tongs to turn them a few times during cooking to make sure they cook evenly. In a fairly gentle heat, they should cook in around 20–30 minutes, depending on their size and the heat of the embers. They are ready when a skewer pierces through the flesh with ease.

To serve, warm the onions through in a pan, then spoon into the sliced-open potatoes. Scatter over the cheese and walnuts and tuck in whilst piping hot.

Other easy fillings...

■ Mozzarella, black olives and a dollop of pesto (see Home-made Pesto on page 37).

■ Flaked tuna and home-made coleslaw.

■ Chilli con carne (see Cowboy Chilli on page 92), with lots of grated Cheddar.

■ Shredded cooked gammon, cooked sliced beetroot and a drizzle of soured cream.

■ Mushrooms sautéed in butter with a little garlic and parsley.

■ Crisp smoked bacon, crumbled goat's cheese and a sprinkle of chopped hazelnuts.

■ Vegetable curry with mint and cucumber yogurt.

bread on the fire

Campfire calzone pizzas

I first got this idea from my friend Liz who is a scout leader and, along with the hot dog ideas on page 79, this is another thing that goes down brilliantly at woodland bonfire-based kids' birthday parties. It's most practical to make the dough at home where you (and any little helpers!) can knead to your heart's content in the knowledge that hands can be easily washed afterwards. The kids can then make their own calzone at your cooking site, adding their favourite toppings before sealing up and laying on the grill to cook.

MAKES 6 CALZONE PIZZAS

For the dough
600g strong white bread flour
1 tsp fine sea salt
1 tsp dried mixed herbs
7g sachet fast-action dried yeast
3 tbsp olive oil, plus extra for greasing
350ml hand-hot water

For the topping
Selection of toppings for people to choose
    from, such as sweetcorn, pepperoni slices,
    chopped ham, flaked tuna, sliced peppers
    or mushrooms, olives, chopped fresh basil
1 x 200g carton passata
2 x 125g balls mozzarella, torn into pieces

You will also need 6 large sheets of foil, lightly oiled on one side.

First make the dough. Add the flour, salt, dried herbs and yeast to a large mixing bowl and stir until evenly mixed. Pour in the oil and hand-hot water, mixing with a wooden spoon until you have a rough, crumbly dough. Add a little more water if it looks too dry, or a little more flour if it looks too wet.

Drizzle a little oil on the worktop, spreading it around with your hands. Tip the dough on to it, then knead well until smooth and stretchy, about 5–8 minutes.

Cut the dough into 6 equal pieces, place each one in the centre of an oiled sheet of foil and loosely fold over the foil to enclose the dough. Pack away in a box with a lid, ready to transport to your cooking site. Prepare a selection of your chosen toppings and pack those away too. The dough will be quite happy at room temperature for a couple of hours; any longer and I would store it in the fridge.

When you are ready to cook, lay out the bowls of toppings, ideally on a camp table, or blanket, and give the kids a package of dough each. Get them to press it out flat into a pizza shape, about 1cm thick. Spread a little passata on one half of each round, leaving a border around the edge, and then top with the mozzarella and whatever else you want. For each calzone, fold the dough in half over the filling and crimp all around the edges to seal the filling inside (as if you were making a pasty).

Loosely fold over the foil again, sealing it completely, and place on the grill over a medium-hot fire, turning over every now and then. Depending on the heat of the fire, they will take around 20–30 minutes to cook. Unfold one carefully to peek inside; it should be crisp and cooked through, not raw and doughy. If not, reseal and cook for another few minutes. Once ready, they will be scorching hot, so let them cool for a few minutes before tucking in.

Bannock bread

This hearty flat bread with Celtic roots is traditionally made in a pan over an open fire. It's a brilliantly easy bread for the campfire and is great eaten hot with either jam, chocolate spread or cream cheese. The milk powder may seem a slightly odd addition but it helps to soften the texture and works with the baking powder to get a slight rise (find milk powder near the UHT milk in the supermarket). Using dried milk for bonfire or campfire cooking is ideal as it means all the dry ingredients are mixed and bagged ready for travel with no chilling required.

Whilst I'm not normally a big fan of the cup measuring system at home, it is quite useful here. I use a measuring cup (250ml) for this bread so I can just scoop the dry ingredients straight into the food bag, then the cup gets chucked in too so I can measure out the water on site. It's pretty forgiving – you could use a tin mug or a jam jar instead. Just get the ratios of flour (2 parts) to oats and milk powder (1 part each) about right.

MAKES 1 LOAF, ENOUGH FOR 2–4 PEOPLE

2 cups (500ml) self-raising flour	1 tsp sea salt
1 cup (250ml) rolled oats	A little vegetable oil, for the pan
1 cup (250ml) dried milk powder	About 1 cup (250ml) cold water
1 tsp baking powder	

You will also need a medium ziplock food bag and a large, heavy-based frying pan.

Measure the flour, oats and milk powder into a ziplock food bag (hang the bag inside a bowl to help keep it open as you measure). Add the baking powder and salt, then seal the bag tightly, squeezing out as much air as you can. Give the bag a shake-about to mix everything evenly.

When you are ready to cook, set a heavy-based frying pan on to the grill over your fire. You can also lay the pan directly on to the glowing embers of a non-flaming, not-too-hot fire. Add a little oil and leave the pan to get hot. Meanwhile, add just less than a cupful of cold water to the dry ingredients in the bag and reseal. Give it all a squish-about using your hands, mixing it together to make a dough. Add a tiny bit more water if it seems dry.

Remove the pan from the fire and rest it on flat ground. Open up the bag and squeeze the dough as best you can into the hot pan, accepting that there will always be a little left over (this is the price you must pay for no kneading and clean hands!). Press the dough firmly down in the pan with a spatula or fish slice, aiming for around 2cm thickness.

Get the pan back over or into the fire and let the dough cook until the underside is crisp and brown. Turn it over (it should be pretty sturdy and easy to do) and cook the other side until golden. At this point, you can move the pan to a cooler area of the fire and keep cooking and turning until the inside is cooked. You need to use your judgement a little here; either lift the bread and tap it with your knuckles (the more hollow it sounds the more cooked it is), or break it open a little to peek inside.

Tear the bread into pieces and serve with your favourite spreadable thing – jam, chocolate spread and garlic cream cheese (not together!) are our favourites.

Frying pan naan bread

Normally made in a very hot clay oven, naan breads work really well when cooked in a frying pan over an open fire. These are brilliant with both the spiced meat recipes below.

MAKES 8 NAAN BREADS

Vegetable oil, for greasing and frying
800g plain flour
7g sachet fast-action dried yeast
2 tbsp nigella (black onion) seeds

2 tsp caster sugar
1 tsp sea salt
About 400ml hand-hot water
2 tbsp plain yogurt

Lightly grease 2 or 3 baking sheets with oil.

Weigh the flour into a mixing bowl, add the yeast, nigella seeds, sugar and salt and mix well. Pour in the hand-hot water and add the yogurt, mixing with a wooden spoon until you have a rough dough.

Drizzle a little oil on the worktop, spreading it around with your hands. Tip the dough on to it, then knead well until smooth and elastic, about 8–10 minutes. Transfer the dough to a clean, lightly oiled mixing bowl, cover with cling film and leave to rise at room temperature for an hour.

Cut the dough into 8 even pieces and flatten out each one into a traditional teardrop shape, about 1cm thick. Lay on the prepared baking sheets, loosely cover with cling film and leave to rise again for 30 minutes.

When you are ready to cook, place a large, flameproof (no plastic handles) frying pan on to the grill over your medium-hot fire and add a splash of oil. Fry the naan breads, two at a time, for a few minutes on each side until golden and crisp on the outside and a little puffed up. Keep them warm whilst you cook the rest.

two spiced meat recipes

For me, spices and fire go naturally together, the warmth of the spices matching the cooking method perfectly, and these recipes are inspired by my favourite Middle Eastern flavours of cumin, turmeric and cinnamon.

Both of these spiced meat recipes are a doddle to prepare in your own kitchen and keep in the fridge, ready for cooking over an open fire or fire pit in your back garden. But if you're in a camper van with a fridge, or on a campsite with access to a fridge, these are great for campsite cooking too; or you can prepare them at home and take with you in a cool box. When handwashing facilities are minimal, it's a great trick to use a pair of latex gloves to mix the meat, thread onto kebabs or shape into burgers.

If you fancy a bit of campfire baking, both the burgers and the kebabs are good served with the Frying Pan Naan Bread above, or for a speedier option simply open up some warmed pitta breads and stuff the meat inside.

Best-ever spiced chicken kebabs

With their gentle spicing, these delicious chicken kebabs are brilliant for introducing children to new spices, and they are insanely popular with my kids and their friends. There is enough here to feed a crowd, but this is an easy recipe to scale down.

MAKES 8–10 LARGE KEBABS

1.2kg skinless, boneless chicken thighs, cut into bite-size pieces (about 1.8kg, if preparing whole thighs yourself)
2 tbsp olive oil
4 cloves garlic, chopped
1 tbsp ground turmeric

1 tbsp cumin seeds
1–2 tsp paprika, or to taste
Sea salt and freshly ground black pepper
Small handful of chopped coriander, to serve

You will also need 8–10 metal or bamboo skewers (if using bamboo they are best soaked in cold water for an hour or so to help prevent them from burning).

In a mixing bowl, combine the chicken pieces, oil, garlic and all the spices, plus a generous grind of black pepper, but no salt just yet. Thread the chicken on to 8–10 long skewers, then place in a large dish or baking tray, cover and leave to marinate in the fridge for an hour, or for up to 24 hours.

Cook on the grill over a hot fire for around 15–20 minutes, turning regularly, until the chicken is cooked through.

When they are cooked, sprinkle with a little salt and scatter on the coriander before serving.

Middle Eastern lamb and date burgers

Even if you think you're not keen on dates I'd urge you to give these a try; the dates add a very subtle sweetness that enhances the spiciness and means you don't really need to add any extra relish or chutney.

MAKES 8 BURGERS

1kg minced lamb
1 onion, very finely chopped or grated
175g stoned dried dates, chopped
1 tbsp cumin seeds, roughly ground
1 tsp ground cinnamon

1 tsp ground turmeric
A pinch of dried chilli flakes, or to taste
Small bunch *each* of coriander and parsley, chopped
Sea salt and freshly ground black pepper

Take a large mixing bowl and simply mix everything together thoroughly, seasoning to taste with salt and black pepper. Divide the mixture into 8 even-size balls and shape into burgers, each around 2cm thick. Place on a large plate, cover and set aside in the fridge for an hour, or for up to 24 hours, to allow the flavours to develop.

When you are ready, lay the burgers on the grill over your medium-hot glowing fire and cook for around 5–6 minutes on each side.

cauldron cooking

The following two recipes get cooked in a Dutch oven hung over the fire. My kids say it looks like a witch's cauldron and so the name has stuck for us!

Rabbit, bacon and pearl barley stew

Cooked in a Dutch oven hung over a glowing fire, this simmering cauldron of comfort certainly looks the part for Halloween feasting. I know eating rabbit is controversial for some – and I've certainly had no luck in persuading my kids to eat rabbit stew – but as a very common wild animal they are perhaps one of the most ethical meats available. Something, I think, that is worth embracing just a little more often, although this dish works very well with jointed chicken too, if you prefer.

SERVES 6

175g pearl barley
3 tbsp plain flour
2 rabbits (wild if possible), jointed
3 tbsp olive oil
2 onions, chopped
3 carrots, chopped
3 sticks celery, chopped
125g (about 6 rashers) smoked streaky
   bacon, chopped

3 sprigs of thyme
500ml chicken stock
Large glass of white wine (about 250ml)
Small bunch of flat-leaf parsley, roughly
   chopped
50g butter
Sea salt and freshly ground black pepper

Begin by soaking the pearl barley in plenty of cold water for an hour before you start cooking the stew.

Sprinkle the flour on to a large plate and season with a little salt and black pepper. Toss the pieces of rabbit, one by one, in the flour so they get an even light coating.

Add the oil to a Dutch oven hung over a high heat, then add the floured rabbit pieces. Fry for a few minutes on each side to seal. Add the onions, carrots, celery, bacon and thyme and fry for a further 10 minutes, stirring from time to time until the vegetables are just starting to colour a little at the edges.

Drain the pearl barley, then add it to the pot along with the stock and wine. Season with a little more salt and black pepper and cover with the lid. Simmer steadily for 1–1½ hours, or until the rabbit is cooked and the pearl barley is tender. Keep half an eye on the stew and if it looks like it's getting a little dry, add a splash of water.

Once cooked, stir through the parsley and butter and let it melt (rabbit is a very lean meat and benefits from a bit of richness by way of a little butter or cream), then add a little more seasoning if necessary. We tend to eat this on its own, but serve it with some crusty bread to accompany if you like.

Cowboy chilli with cornbread dumplings

Whilst I've never met a real cowboy, I feel like this might be just the sort of thing cowboys would enjoy eating out in the wild. It's certainly a big hit in our house and was first cooked in the back garden on an early autumn evening, proving you really don't need to travel very far to bring a bit of adventure into your life.

SERVES 4

For the chilli
2 tbsp olive oil
2 red onions, chopped
2 large red peppers, deseeded and chopped
1 tbsp cumin seeds
1–2 tsp dried chilli flakes, or to taste
500g minced beef
4 tomatoes (or use 1 x 400g tin chopped tomatoes in place of both the fresh tomatoes and passata)
3 cloves garlic, chopped
1 x 200g carton passata

1 x 400g tin kidney beans, drained and rinsed
500ml beef stock
Sea salt and freshly ground black pepper

For the cornbread dumplings
200g self-raising flour
80g quick-cook polenta
50g shredded vegetable or beef suet
125–150ml cold water

To serve (optional)
3–4 spring onions, chopped
Small bunch of coriander, chopped

First make the chilli. Add the oil, onions, red peppers, cumin seeds and chilli flakes to a Dutch oven hung high over your fire, then cook over a moderately gentle heat for around 30 minutes until the vegetables are starting to colour a little. Increase the heat by lowering the oven so it's nearer to the coals and then add the minced beef, stirring occasionally to break it up as it lightly caramelizes – this will take 10–15 minutes.

Add the tomatoes and garlic, stir-frying for about 5 minutes, then stir in the passata, kidney beans and stock, and season with salt and black pepper. Cover with the lid, raise the oven up a little so the heat is more gentle and simmer steadily for 30 minutes.

Whilst the chilli is cooking, make the cornbread dumplings. If you are cooking in your back garden these are very simple to make in the comfort of your kitchen – just mix everything together in a bowl to make a fairly stiff dough. If not, I suggest mixing all the dry ingredients together in a food bag before you head off to your cooking site. Then you can simply add the water into the bag and mix together, in much the same way as for the Bannock Bread on page 86.

Divide the dough into 8 evenish pieces, then drop into the bubbling chilli, allowing the dumplings to sit on the surface. Re-cover and cook at a steady simmer for another 30 minutes until they are risen and springy to the touch. To check they are done, simply pierce one with a skewer; it should come out clean. Serve sprinkled with spring onions and coriander, if you like.

classic bonfire treats

Campfire popcorn, sweet and savoury

This is a great treat for a forest-based birthday party. As the heat from a real fire can be fierce, you need to keep an eye out for burning the kernels before they pop.

MAKES A BIG PANFUL, ENOUGH FOR AROUND 6–8 PEOPLE
2 tbsp vegetable oil
150g popcorn kernels

Pour the oil into a big, fireproof (no plastic handles) saucepan with a lid and set it on the grill over your fire. Add the popcorn kernels and shake to coat them in oil. Put the lid on tight and wait until the popping starts – this can happen quite quickly or it may take longer, depending on the heat your fire is giving out. Using a thick, dry tea towel to protect you from the heat, shake the pan from side to side every now and then. And occasionally lift the lid a fraction to see if you can smell any whiff of burning – if you do then move the pan to a slightly cooler area of your fire.

Once the popping has stopped, it's ready and you can simply sprinkle in sugar or salt to taste, or try one of the flavours below. The Jerk-spiced savoury popcorn is probably more of a grown-up flavour and a great snack with a cold beer too!

Flavouring your popcorn

You can't beat simple sugar for a sweet tooth, or salt for a savoury one, but here are a couple of other things to flavour your popcorn with…

- **Toffee popcorn sauce** Put 70g soft brown sugar, 50g butter, 3 tablespoons golden syrup and a pinch of sea salt into a small pan and bring to a simmer on your hob. Boil for a minute, then pour into an enamel camping mug or small pan ready for reheating over the fire whilst the popcorn is cooking.

  Whilst the corn is popping, simply set the mug over a coolish part of the fire where it will melt as it reheats. Once the corn has all popped, pour in the sauce and stir well. Leave it to cool for a minute or two before trying to eat it, as it will be very hot.

- **Jerk-spiced savoury popcorn** Put 2 teaspoons *each* dried thyme, dried chilli flakes, garlic powder, soft dark brown sugar and sea salt flakes into a jam jar, along with 1 teaspoon *each* ground allspice and freshly ground black pepper, plus ½ teaspoon ground cinnamon. Shake together to mix well, then sprinkle over the freshly popped hot popcorn.

A couple of other classics…

I don't think Bonfire Night would be complete without marshmallows and toffee apples, and I have a whole raft of childhood memories involving both. Most are joyous, but one is not so positive – my worst kitchen accident ever involved a large blob of molten toffee on my index finger, and the scar from the resulting burn is still visible today. So, parents, I would urge you to make these for your kids rather than with them, and then let them enjoy the finished results unscathed.

Toffee apples

MAKES 6

6 medium eating apples, thoroughly washed and dried, any stalks removed
400g caster sugar

4 tbsp golden syrup
100ml cold water

You will also need 6 lolly sticks (easily found in cook shops).

Pierce the top of the apples with the tip of a knife and insert a lolly stick firmly into the centre of each. Lay a sheet of non-stick baking paper on a baking tray and set it near your stove, spreading the apples out on it.

Weigh the sugar into a heavy-based saucepan, then add the syrup and water. Set the pan over a medium heat, stirring until the sugar has dissolved completely, then bring to the boil. Set a sugar thermometer in the pan and boil steadily until the 'hard crack' stage (149°C) is reached. If you don't have a sugar thermometer, have a glass of cold water at the ready. It's difficult to be precise about times as it depends on the heat source, but after about 8 minutes of boiling, drop a little toffee mixture into the glass. It should harden immediately and be brittle once you remove it from the water. If it's still squidgy, then boil for a further couple of minutes before testing again.

When the toffee is ready, turn off the heat. Take one apple at a time, and holding it firmly by the stick, dip and roll it quickly and carefully in the toffee until it's completely covered. Place back on the baking tray and repeat with the other apples. Leave the toffee to cool and set, then get stuck in. (There will be a little more toffee than you need, so simply pour the leftovers into a non-stick baking tray, leave to set, then break into pieces and eat separately.)

Gingernut s'mores

A s'more is an American bonfire classic where you melt a marshmallow then sandwich it between two sweet crackers, sometimes with a square of chocolate too. Or you can, of course, simply toast marshmallows on long forks, and this is enduringly popular with kids. But how about a marshmallow melted between two gingernuts? A little spicy, hugely sticky and very moreish…

All you need, per person, is two **gingernut biscuits** and a big **marshmallow** to put between them. Wrap each biscuit sandwich snugly in foil and slide on to the grill over your fire or into the low glowing embers of the fire. Leave to cook for just a few minutes, turning over once or twice, until the marshmallow has melted.

I should also say you can use whatever type of biscuit you like – we've had quite a bit of success with Jaffa cake marshmallow sandwiches (just make sure the chocolate faces inwards, and be prepared for a little extra stickiness!).

sugar and spice

Just as with savoury things and fire cooking, sweet things cooked over or eaten around a fire are also best, to my mind, with the addition of a little spiciness. It's just a combination that works.

Sticky gingerbread

This old-fashioned gingerbread is one of my all-time favourite cakes and one that my mum used to make often when we were kids. She used to either top it with sesame seeds or sharp lemony icing and, as I can't decide which I like best, here I have opted for both. This rich and spicy cake feels like just the right thing to eat around Bonfire Night or Halloween, and as a bonus it gets better after a day or two of storing, so it's a good one to make ahead. To store, wrap in foil or keep in an airtight tin. It will keep well for about a week.

MAKES 1 CAKE, ENOUGH FOR 9–12 PIECES

350g self-raising flour	150g black treacle
1 heaped tbsp ground ginger	300ml milk
1 tsp bicarbonate of soda	2 eggs
150g butter, plus extra for greasing	25g sesame seeds
150g soft dark brown sugar	5 tbsp icing sugar
150g golden syrup	About 1 tbsp lemon juice

Preheat the oven to 180°C/Gas 4. Lightly grease (and line if it's a bit of a sticker) a 24–25cm square cake tin.

Weigh the flour into a large mixing bowl, add the ginger and bicarbonate of soda and stir to mix thoroughly.

Put the butter, brown sugar, syrup, treacle and milk into a saucepan and set over a medium heat. Bring to the boil, stirring frequently, until the butter has melted and everything is combined. Pour into the mixing bowl with the flour mixture and beat well until smooth, then crack in both eggs and beat again.

Pour into the prepared tin, spreading evenly, then sprinkle over the sesame seeds. Bake in the oven for around 30–35 minutes until springy to the touch. A metal skewer inserted into the centre should come out clean.

Leave to cool slightly in the tin, then transfer from the tin to a wire rack and cool completely. Once cold, mix the icing sugar with just enough lemon juice to give a good drizzling consistency. Drizzle the icing over the top of the cake and leave to set before cutting into squares.

Fire-baked stuffed apples with spiced fruit and nuts

This delicious warming pudding is the perfect autumn treat and it is a breeze to make in the glowing embers of a fire. The double layer of foil not only protects the apples from burning, it also ensures that none of the delicious juices are lost.

SERVES 4

75g dried apricots, chopped
75g dried stoned prunes, chopped
30g pecans, chopped
30g soft dark brown sugar
1 tsp ground mixed spice
Generous 1 tbsp golden syrup

Finely grated zest and juice of ½ lemon
4 large eating apples
25g butter, cut into 4 pieces
Crème fraîche or double cream, to serve
   (optional)

In a small bowl, mix together the apricots, prunes, pecans, brown sugar and mixed spice, until the sugar evenly coats everything. Drizzle in the syrup and add the lemon zest and juice, stirring until evenly mixed.

Core the apples (keeping them whole), creating about a 2cm-wide or so hole down through the centre of each one right the way to the bottom. Use a small sharp knife to score a line gently around the middle of each apple (this stops it bursting as it cooks), then lay each one on a generous square of foil. Spoon the filling into the holes, pushing it well down to the bottom. Top each with a piece of butter and wrap tightly in the foil, then wrap each apple in a second layer of foil before placing into the glowing embers of the fire.

Cook for around 20–25 minutes, using tongs to turn occasionally, until the apples are cooked. To test, remove one from the fire and squeeze through the foil using a tea towel to protect your hands. If it is soft and yielding to the touch it is done. If not, return to the fire and cook for a further 5 minutes or so.

Give everyone their own wrapped apple on a plate, and serve whilst piping hot, perhaps with a dollop of crème fraîche or a drizzle of cream.

Luscious vanilla rice pudding

I make this warming rice pudding in my Dutch oven hung over the fire pit, where it takes a couple of hours of gentle puttering away to thicken to a creamy consistency, with pretty much no attention bar the odd stir towards the end of cooking. You could also do it in an old saucepan (avoid plastic handles) resting on a coolish part of the grill set over the fire; it will cook slightly quicker and need a little more stirring to stop the bottom burning.

SERVES ABOUT 4 (DEPENDING ON GREED AND HOW CHILLY YOU ARE)

1 litre milk

150g pudding rice

60g granulated sugar

50g butter

1 tsp vanilla extract

You will also need a medium ziplock food bag. Open up the food bag and rest it inside a mixing bowl, hooking the top of the bag over the rim of the bowl to stop it falling down. Slowly pour in the milk, then set the bowl on kitchen scales and weigh in the rice, sugar and butter. Finally, add the vanilla extract, then seal up the bag, squeezing out as much air as possible. Give the bag a little squash and squeeze to get everything nicely mixed.

At this point I usually put the bag inside my Dutch oven before transporting it to my fire's destination. When you are ready to cook (and I suggest getting it on early as good rice pudding takes time), simply open up the ziplock bag and empty the contents into the Dutch oven or pan. Cover tightly with the lid and hang the Dutch oven high over the fire where the pudding should cook to perfection in around 2 hours (stir it occasionally towards the end of cooking).

Once the rice is tender and surrounded by a thick creamy sauce, spoon into bowls or mugs and tuck in.

Some other ways to flavour your pudding...

This rice pudding is fab simply flavoured with vanilla, but there are other things I sometimes try, to ring the changes:

- Replace the vanilla with rose water. Take a handful of roughly chopped pistachios in a food bag to sprinkle over before you serve.

- Leave out the vanilla and add 1 teaspoon ground mixed spice and a handful of raisins to the bag before sealing. You could also add a splash of sherry or whisky to the bag as well.

- Replace 400ml of the milk with 1 x 400ml tin of coconut milk, and add the finely grated zest of 2 limes to the bag before sealing.

and something warm to drink...

It's always a good idea to have an easy warming drink on standby that you can heat through and hand out to your guests when things start to get a little chilly.

Warming spiced apple punch

This simple mulled apple punch will warm hands and tummies alike. Grown-ups could always add a little splash of rum for the extra warming effect it brings!

SERVES ABOUT 8

2 litres cloudy apple juice
4 clementines, sliced into discs (peel left on)
3–4 tbsp runny honey, or to taste
4 star anise

2 cinnamon sticks
1 tsp whole cloves
A little rum, to taste (optional)

Pour the apple juice into an old fireproof (no plastic handles) saucepan and set over a medium heat. Drop the clementine slices into the pan, along with the honey, to taste. Add the star anise, cinnamon sticks and cloves and bring to the boil. Remove from the heat, cover and leave to infuse for at least an hour.

When you are ready to serve, place the pan on the grill over your fire and reheat gently. Taste for sweetness, adding more honey if necessary. Add a splash of rum to taste, if using, then ladle into mugs or heatproof glasses.

Cinnamon and brandy hot chocolate

You can prepare this intensely chocolatey drink ahead of time, so that it's completely low-fuss when the fire is lit. If you are making it for kids (minus the brandy), you may want to replace half the dark chocolate with milk chocolate for a slightly less intense flavour.

SERVES ABOUT 8

2 litres milk
150ml single cream
200g dark chocolate, chopped into small pieces
6 tbsp soft dark brown sugar

4 tbsp good-quality cocoa powder
1 tsp vanilla extract
1 tsp ground cinnamon
A pinch of sea salt
Brandy, to taste

Simply add everything, except the brandy, to a large, fireproof (no plastic handles) saucepan, then cover and set aside until you are ready to serve.

Once your fire is lit and you are ready to drink, set the pan on the grill over the fire and warm through, stirring often, until the chocolate has melted and the mixture comes to just below boiling point. Add brandy to taste, stirring well to mix, then ladle into mugs or heatproof glasses.

CAMP
COOKOUT

Introduction

For the 'full monty' cooking-and-eating-outside experience, camping has got to be the way forward and it's one of my favourite things to do with my family during the summer months. Not only is it a pretty cheap way to holiday, I love the full submergence into nature and the enforced change of pace that camping brings.

What with late bedtimes usually followed by early starts, there never seems to be *quite* enough sleep going on, but for me camping trips are rejuvenating for all sorts of other reasons. I think it's possibly the freedom and the dropping of normal routines that I enjoy most. I have never really been a content follower of regulations and I relish the fact that 'camp rules' bear little resemblance to 'home rules'. Clocks rarely dictate either feeding time or bedtime; you eat when you're hungry and you sleep when you're tired. The kids generally fall into their beds happily when they have exhausted themselves running wild, usually taking the dogs with them to provide some lovely snuggly warmth that would be totally outlawed at home.

As ever, having plenty of nice things to eat always ups the contentment factor, and when your kitchen is outside, the cooking itself becomes very much a communal process and is all the more enjoyable for it. This chapter celebrates the shared act of cooking in the fresh air with friends and family, be it on the beach after a day mucking about in the water, or around a fire back at the campsite. Here you will find easy, sociable recipes that are designed to extend the fun of the day well into the night, plus a few pretty much instant dinner tricks that will be invaluable to have up your sleeve when you are too tired to make much of an effort, or for when the weather is rather more inclement than is desirable.

CAMP COOKING GEAR

The first thing I should do here is to hold my hand up high and confess that I don't really do 'wild camping'. With two kids and two dogs in tow, there isn't a hope in hell of getting all that we need to take in a backpack, or even several backpacks. Besides, I like my duvet and pillow rather too much for that. No, my school of camping involves opening up the boot and chucking stuff in until it's rammed full of useful things. But I do like to head to campsites with very minimal facilities, one whiff of a 'clubhouse' and I'm off, which is another good reason for 'packing large' – I know that I have everything I need to make everyone happy and comfortable. If you're less constrained by circumstances and the desire for comfort, and backpacker camping is your bag, then I direct you to the Wilderness Eats chapter for lots of easy-to-carry ideas.

There are two main ways I cook when I'm camping. The first, and my preferred way for the sheer 'primeval-ness' of it, is over a fire pit with both a grill and a Dutch oven hung from a tripod over the top (some fire pits will have the grill placed directly on it; mine hangs over the fire). Fire pits are brilliant as they raise the fire off the ground and most campsites allow them as the fire is neatly and safely contained, and once you hang the grill over it you are essentially making

a barbecue on which to cook. See the Bonfire Celebrations introduction on page 76 for info on these bits of kit. Second, cooking on a camping stove fuelled by a gas bottle, which is essential for making a quick morning brew or for cooking up a speedy meal when it's too nippy or damp to linger around a campfire.

OTHER USEFUL STUFF...

We have a fold-up kitchen shelf unit that felt just a bit too middle-aged when we bought it many years ago, but it's proved really very useful in the long run. It's a great thing for raising your gas stove off the ground, so is especially good if you've got young children, and it also means you are cooking at standing height which is very practical. There is plenty of storage room underneath too. We also have a fold-out camping picnic bench that has proved invaluable for keeping food out of the way and off the ground. If, like us, you have dogs, you will know without me even saying that this is what is known as 'a good thing'.

A cool box is pretty much essential and, providing you have a few freezer blocks, it will keep perishables chilled for a long weekend, which is how long we usually camp for. If you are planning a longer trip, some campsites have a freezer tucked away so you can refreeze your blocks to keep your food fresh for longer. Sometimes I travel with well-wrapped frozen meat in the cool box too, where it defrosts slowly over a couple of days before I cook it. If your cool box is half-full, scrunch up a few sheets of newspaper to tuck in the top to keep it packed full and more efficient.

In terms of other essentials, I wouldn't dream of leaving for a camping trip without my ever-useful box of tricks or my fireproof pots and pans – see the Bonfire Celebrations introduction on page 78. In fact, pretty much all the advice I offer there in terms of essential gear will come in handy here too. And don't forget a roll of foil (a double layer of foil lining any roasting or baking tin makes washing-up a breeze).

As also discussed in the Bonfire Celebrations chapter, cooking over real fire is an art rather than a science, and as such it's impossible for me to give precise cooking times. This kind of cooking is more about trusting your instincts than it is about following the rules, which is probably why I love it so much. Regarding the cooking temperature of your fire, the hand-heat test in Barbecue Feast on page 43 is a good guide for open fires too.

GETTING AHEAD

With many of the recipes you will see that I suggest mixing and bagging up dry ingredients at home. This means you aren't taking along endless containers of herbs, spices or staples. It also means because the ingredients are at ambient temperature, you are not tied to eating a certain recipe at any time – they will sit happily until the night you feel like it. This mixing at home idea is one I also use for marinating meat, such as with the Quick Campfire Beef Curry with Spiced Roast Potatoes (see page 115) or the sumptuous Overnight Pulled Pork (see page 118), although of course you will then need to store the marinated meat in a cool box until you cook it.

A SHARP KNIFE...

A golden rule for me when camping is to make things as easy as possible on the cooking front, hence the getting organized at home bit. It also means that on the campsite, vegetables are cut rough and rustic (this is not the place for neat chopping). Even with the sharpest of knives you are likely to be chopping on a wobbly camping table at best, or possibly even on the ground. So on the subject of knives, take a really sharp one with you, wrapped safely in a couple of tea towels and bound tight with a rubber band. It really is your most important friend in the kitchen and I wouldn't dream of going camping without my trusty sharp knife.

AND LASTLY – KEEP WARM ANY WHICH WAY YOU CAN!

If I were to offer one piece of advice to a novice camper, it would be to take more, much more, stuff than you think you need to keep warm. If everyone is toasty and snug, with nice food in their tummies, then the camping experience will be a far happier one. I have a large reindeer skin that I take, without fail, on camping trips, using it as a blanket in the evenings and to sleep on at night. A by-product of the meat industry in Finland, this ethical hide rug was a bit of an extravagance, but one that I feel was entirely justified given that it makes the most comfortable bed I have ever slept on.

speedy ideas

Spice it up!

When you are camping, you can't really go wrong with simply grilling meat, fish or vegetables (and you'll find plenty of ideas in the Barbecue Feast chapter that will work well on the campsite too). But the best and simplest way I know to boost flavour is by adding a little spice into the equation, either before you grill as a dry rub, or by sprinkling a little over the cooked food, just as you would season to taste with salt and pepper. There are some brilliant ready-mixed spice blends out there and having a tub or two of your favourite ones packed away with your camp gear will be endlessly useful.

Some of my favourite spice blends are:

- **Ras el hanout** – a Moroccan blend of many spices including cumin, coriander, cinnamon and chilli, and sometimes even dried rose petals.

- **Jamaican jerk** – hot with chilli, but also fragrant with other spices including allspice, thyme and nutmeg.

- **Garam masala** – an Indian blend of spices including coriander, cumin, cardamom, cloves and ginger or cinnamon.

- **Harissa** – a pungent Middle Eastern blend of spices including dried red chillies, cumin, caraway and coriander.

Grilled aubergines with olive oil and spice seasoning

This is possibly the best way ever to devour an aubergine. Cook whole unpricked **aubergines** directly on the grill over your fire until lightly charred all over and really soft and squidgy, about 30–35 minutes, depending on the heat. Cut in half through the middle and open up like a baked potato, then drizzle in plenty of **extra virgin olive oil** and season with sea salt and freshly ground black pepper. Then add a sprinkle of **spice magic** (see previous page for a few spice blend ideas). Aubergines work especially well with any spice blend containing cumin.

Grilled sweetcorn with flavoured butters

For **chilli and coriander sweetcorn**, cut 2 **cobs of corn** (without leaves) in half and put each one in the middle of a square of foil. In a small bowl, beat together around 40g softened **butter** with 1 tablespoon **chopped coriander**, a pinch of **dried chilli flakes** and a little sea salt and freshly ground black pepper. Spread all over the sweetcorn, then wrap up tightly in the foil. Cook on the grill over the fire for around 20 minutes until soft. Serve in the foil for people to open themselves, rolling the corn in the melted butter as you eat.

Other flavoured butters to try...

All these flavoured butters can be mixed at home and then packed in tubs in your cool box where they will keep for several days.

- **Smoked paprika and garlic** – mix ½ teaspoon smoked paprika and 1 crushed clove of garlic into the butter, season to taste with sea salt and black pepper.
- **Parsley and caper** – finely chop 1 tablespoon flat-leaf parsley and mix it with the butter, along with a heaped teaspoon of chopped (drained) capers. Season to taste with sea salt and black pepper.

Chargrilled broad beans

This is a ridiculously easy thing to do with a bag of fresh broad beans in their pods. Simply tip the pods directly on to the grill over your fire and spread out in a single layer. Let them cook on one side until lightly charred, then turn over and cook on the other side – depending on the heat, this will take around 5 minutes each side.

To serve, pile them on to a plate and dig in – simply open up each pod, pick out the beans and pop them in your mouth. Little dishes of olive oil, sea salt and cracked black pepper to dip them in make these simple beans taste just sublime.

Forks on sticks for marshmallows and sausages

Get a handful of cheap forks (try rummaging around a charity shop) and fix them securely to the top of long bamboo sticks with tightly wound wire. A few of these tucked into your camping gear will be much appreciated by your kids when it comes to toasting large marshmallows around the campfire.

Or what about sticking fat sausages on to the forks? Held over a fire, and turned regularly, these are great for slightly older kids to cook themselves.

Sardines on sticks

You can cook fresh whole (gutted) sardines on forks, just like the sausages, or how about threading them on to sturdy twigs that you impale into the sand or soil so they sit over the fire? Simply rotate the sticks a few times during cooking so they cook evenly. Grilled sardines need little to accompany them bar a grind of black pepper and a generous pinch of sea salt.

Mussels with cider and sage

This is an ideal first night camping supper – something easy to cook over the fire after a long and tedious journey, followed by a frenetic, and possibly fractious, setting up of camp. As always with camping, the trick to their ease is to prepare a little at home before you leave. This recipe serves 2, but it is easily doubled if there are more of you, or if your kids are rather more adventurous than mine.

Wash and de-beard 1kg fresh **mussels** (in shells) at home (discarding any open ones), then bung them in a large ziplock food bag. Add 2 finely chopped **shallots**, 1 chopped clove **garlic** and a small handful of chopped **sage**. Season well with sea salt and freshly ground black pepper, before sealing the bag up tightly and packing at the top of your cool box so it's easy to find.

Then once the tent is up, the campfire is glowing, and you have a glass of something nice on the go, you can get them ready to cook. Take 4 sheets of foil, lay one on top of the other in a cross shape, then repeat with the other 2. Divide the mussel mixture between the 2 foil crosses, piling it into the centre of each. Bring up the sides to create walls, pour a good glass of **dry cider** (about 150ml) into each, then seal each top tightly to make a foil bag. You don't need to compact the bags really tightly, a little space between the foil and mussels is good as it allows the steam to circulate efficiently.

Wrap a final sheet of foil around each bag to make sure it's completely sealed, place on the grill over the fire and cook for 20–30 minutes until the mussels are open and cooked (discard any that remain closed once cooked). Turn the parcels over halfway through cooking so they cook evenly. Serve a bag per person, with plenty of crusty bread to dunk in the lovely juices as you go.

pasta – a campsite lifesaver!

Easy to carry and quick to cook, dried pasta was possibly invented for camping trips, plus there are endless variations of easy sauces that can be knocked up with as much or as little effort as you can muster. Often the simplest sauces are the best, so here are a few ideas for tasty dinners that can be created with not a lot of ingredients.

Each recipe uses a 500g bag of dried pasta, cooked on a camping stove according to the packet directions until al dente, then drained. All these recipes serve 4 generously.

Asparagus, pecorino and black pepper

I would use penne for this simple late spring dish, cutting the asparagus a similar size to the pasta for easy eating. If you haven't got pecorino, Parmesan is great too.

2 bunches of asparagus, woody ends
   trimmed, cut into bite-size pieces
75g butter, cut into cubes
100g pecorino or Parmesan cheese,
   freshly grated

2–3 tsp cracked black peppercorns,
   or to taste
Sea salt flakes, to taste

In the biggest pan you can get hold of, cook the pasta until it has around 5 minutes to go, then drop in the asparagus and keep cooking until it is just tender. If you haven't got a pan big enough to cook them together, cook separately.

Once the pasta and asparagus are cooked, drain and tip back into the pan. Working quickly whilst they're piping hot, add the butter, pecorino and plenty of cracked black pepper and toss together until the butter and cheese have melted. Season to taste with salt flakes and serve immediately.

Tuna, sweetcorn and Cheddar

An almost instant dinner and a great favourite with my kids, I usually pep up my bowlful with a shake of chilli sauce. Any pasta shape works well here.

2 x 200g tins tuna, ideally packed in olive
   oil, drained
1 x 326g tin sweetcorn, drained
Small bunch of flat-leaf parsley, chopped

100g mature Cheddar cheese, grated
Olive oil, sea salt and freshly ground black
   pepper, to taste

Simply stir everything through the hot freshly cooked pasta, drizzling in oil to taste and seasoning with salt and black pepper. Serve immediately.

Puttanesca

A punchy tomato sauce with olives, capers, anchovies and chilli, this is perfect with spaghetti.

2 tbsp olive oil
3 cloves garlic, chopped
½–1 tsp dried chilli flakes, or to taste
2 x 400g tins chopped tomatoes
A squeeze of tomato purée or tomato ketchup
2 tbsp capers, drained and rinsed

2 tbsp pitted black olives, roughly chopped
1 x 50g tin anchovy fillets in oil, drained and roughly chopped
Sea salt and freshly ground black pepper
Freshly grated Parmesan cheese and torn basil leaves, to serve (optional)

Heat the oil in a large pan and fry the garlic with the chilli flakes for a minute or two. Add the tomatoes and tomato purée or ketchup and bring to a steady simmer, then cook over a medium heat to a thick, almost jam-like consistency, stirring occasionally. This will take about 15–20 minutes.

Stir in the capers, olives and anchovies and cook for a further couple of minutes. Season to taste with salt and black pepper and then stir through the hot freshly cooked pasta. Serve piping hot, ideally sprinkled generously with Parmesan and basil.

Bacon, beetroot and capers

Ready-cooked un-vinegary beetroot in vacuum packs is a really useful thing to have tucked in your camping box – it lasts for ages and doesn't need to be kept in the fridge. It's great for pepping up a dull salad or a sandwich, but it's also very good in hot dishes, particularly when paired with something salty to balance its natural sweetness – here I've used a classic combo of bacon, capers and goat's cheese.

2 tbsp olive oil
12 rashers smoked streaky bacon, roughly chopped
2 x 250g packs ready-cooked beetroot (un-vinegared), roughly sliced

3 tbsp capers, roughly chopped
A bunch of flat-leaf parsley, chopped
200g soft (rindless) goat's cheese, crumbled
Salt and freshly ground black pepper, to taste

Heat up the oil in a frying pan and fry the bacon over a medium-high heat until crisp. Add the beetroot, capers and parsley and stir until hot, adding a splash more oil if it looks a little dry. Stir into the hot cooked pasta and season to taste with salt and freshly ground black pepper. Scatter over the goat's cheese just before serving.

Pepper, chorizo and goat's cheese

A Mediterranean feast of big flavours, perfect with any type of pasta shape.

3 tbsp olive oil
3 peppers (whatever colour you fancy; a mixture looks good), deseeded and roughly chopped
1 x 225g chorizo ring, chopped

3 cloves garlic, chopped
A pinch of dried chilli flakes, or to taste (optional)
200g soft (rindless) goat's cheese, crumbled
Sea salt and freshly ground black pepper

Heat the oil in a large frying pan, add the peppers and chorizo and stir-fry over a medium-high heat for around 15 minutes until the peppers are soft and lightly charred in places.

Add the garlic and chilli flakes, if using, and fry for another minute. Turn off the heat, season to taste with salt and black pepper, then stir through the hot freshly cooked pasta. Sprinkle some goat's cheese over each serving.

Caramelized onion, smoked salmon and cream cheese

This dish was made off the cuff with ingredients I found in a corner shop by our campsite. Take your time with the onions – they add the depth of flavour that makes this special. Spaghetti was my choice with this sauce, but pretty much any pasta will be just fine.

2 tbsp olive oil
2 large onions, sliced
1 tsp dried mixed herbs
1 x 200g tub cream cheese (full-fat or light, as you wish)

180–200g smoked salmon, shredded (skinless smoked mackerel fillets are a good substitute; smoked salmon trimmings are also ideal)
Lemon juice, sea salt and freshly ground black pepper, to taste

Heat the oil in a large frying pan, add the onions and dried herbs and cook gently for at least 30 minutes, stirring occasionally, until soft and tender. Increase the heat slightly and allow the onions to caramelize a little, about another 5–10 minutes.

Add the cream cheese and stir until melted. Stir through the smoked salmon, then add lemon juice, salt and black pepper to taste. Stir through the hot freshly cooked pasta and serve immediately.

fireside feasts

Quick campfire beef curry with spiced roast potatoes

Curry tastes so much nicer if you mix your own spices, but of course if that's too much of a faff, a good curry paste is an acceptable alternative. The beef will be very happy sitting in the dry spices for a couple of days, so for this easy dish I mix the spices and marinate the meat in an ever-trusty ziplock food bag at home, ready to fling in the frying pan at the campsite when I'm ready to cook.

SERVES 2 (EASILY SCALED UP FOR A CROWD)

For the beef curry
3 green cardamom pods, left whole
1 tsp fennel seeds
1 tsp dried chilli flakes
½ tsp black peppercorns
½ tsp ground turmeric
½ tsp ground cinnamon
½ tsp ground ginger
400g skirt steak, sliced across the grain into 5mm strips
1 tbsp vegetable oil

1 red onion, sliced
2 cloves garlic, chopped
1 x 160ml tin coconut cream

For the spiced roast potatoes
400g new potatoes, scrubbed and cut into wedges
1 tsp cumin seeds
2 cloves garlic, chopped
1 tbsp sunflower oil
Sea salt and freshly ground black pepper

For the beef curry, add the cardamom pods, fennel seeds, chilli flakes and peppercorns to a spice mill and grind roughly (or use a pestle and mortar). Tip into a ziplock food bag and add the turmeric, cinnamon and ginger, shaking the bag to mix them all together. Add the beef strips and toss about to coat evenly in the spices. Seal up the bag tightly and pack away in a cool box.

When you're ready to cook, start the potatoes first. Tear off two sheets of foil and lay one on top of the other in a cross shape. Pile the potatoes in the middle, sprinkle on the cumin seeds, garlic and oil and season with salt and black pepper. Seal up tightly into a parcel and place on the grill over your fire pit or barbecue. Cook over a medium heat for around 30 minutes, using tongs to turn the bag over a couple of times to ensure even cooking.

When the potatoes are nearly done, begin the curry either on the grill over a fire pit, or on a camping gas stove. Heat the oil in a frying pan over a medium-low heat, add the onion and fry for about 10 minutes until starting to soften. Stir through the garlic, then tip in the spiced beef mixture, stir-frying over a high heat until colouring in places and cooked to your liking. Season with salt and black pepper, pour in the coconut cream, then stir for a few minutes until heated through. Serve the beef curry spooned over the potatoes.

Warming spiced dhal

A great get-it-ready-at-home dish (just fry up a couple of onions and add water before cooking), this dhal is the perfect warming dish for when the sun goes down and there's a distinct nip in the air. This is ideal served alongside the Quick Campfire Beef Curry with Spiced Roast Potatoes (see previous page), and it's also a good one with kebabs – try it with the Best-ever Spiced Chicken Kebabs (see page 88) and Frying Pan Naan Bread (see page 87).

SERVES 4–6

200g red lentils
2 tsp ground coriander
2 tsp cumin seeds
½–1 tsp dried chilli flakes, or to taste
½ tsp ground turmeric
1 cinnamon stick, broken into 2 or 3 pieces
2 bay leaves
2 onions, peeled

2 tbsp vegetable oil
2 cloves garlic, chopped

To finish
Generous knob of butter
Sea salt and garam masala, to taste
A little chopped coriander (optional)

Get ready at home by hanging a ziplock food bag in a bowl set on kitchen scales. Measure in the lentils, then add all the spices and bay leaves. Seal up the bag, squeezing out as much air as possible, then pack it away with the rest of your food.

When you are ready to cook, roughly chop the onions and add them to an old fireproof (no plastic handles) saucepan along with the oil. Rest on the grill over your fire and cook, stirring occasionally, until soft and lightly golden, about 10–15 minutes. Depending on how fierce your fire is, you may need to move the pan around a bit to find a coolish area so they don't burn before softening.

Add the garlic and stir for a few seconds before tipping in the contents of your ziplock food bag. Stir well, then pour in enough cold water to come about 2cm above the top of the lentils. Bring to a simmer, cover with a lid or snug-fitting piece of foil and let the lentils cook until they are collapsing. This will take about 30–40 minutes, depending on the heat of your fire. Check every 10 minutes or so, giving the lentils a good stir, and add a splash more water as necessary if they are getting too dry. Conversely, take off the lid and cook uncovered if they need thickening up a bit.

When the dhal is ready, remove from the heat, fish out the bay leaves and pieces of cinnamon stick, then stir through a generous knob of butter. Season to taste with salt and a sprinkling of garam masala. A little chopped coriander is great too if you happen to have any lying around!

Peppers stuffed with couscous, dates and blue cheese

These stuffed peppers are cooked in a Dutch oven and they make a filling vegetarian main course or side dish to accompany some grilled meat or fish. To make them easy to lift out of the oven when cooked, rest each pepper on a square of foil that you scrunch up around the sides a little so each is encased separately (see the photo on page 109).

SERVES 6

350g couscous
100g stoned dried dates, chopped
60g toasted pine nuts
1 tsp vegetable stock powder
A pinch of dried chilli flakes, or to taste

6 large peppers (whatever colour you fancy; a mixture looks good)
25g butter or 2 tbsp olive oil
150g soft blue cheese, such as St Agur or Gorgonzola, cut into 6 equal pieces
Sea salt and freshly ground black pepper

Get the couscous filling ready before you leave home. Hang a ziplock food bag in a bowl and set the bowl on kitchen scales. Measure in the couscous, then add the dates, pine nuts, stock powder and chilli flakes and season with salt and black pepper. Give the bag a shake-about to mix it up, then seal it, squeezing out as much air as possible. Pack along with the rest of your food.

When you are ready to cook, slice the top off each pepper and scoop out the seeds, reserving the tops as lids. Tear off 6 squares of foil and wrap a piece around the base of each pepper before lining them up inside a Dutch oven. Shake up the bag of couscous to mix it again and then divide evenly between the peppers – you want each pepper to be around two-thirds full, so if your peppers are on the small side you may have a little leftover couscous (if so, simply seal up the bag again; it will keep quite happily for another time).

Top the couscous with dots of butter or a drizzle of oil, then add a piece of blue cheese. Pour cold water into each pepper so it just comes to the level of the couscous, then pop the lids back on. Put the lid on the oven and hang it over your fire (you're aiming for medium heat). Use tongs to put a few hot coals, around 8–10, on the lid to cook the peppers from the top as well. Cook until the peppers are soft and tender, around an hour or so.

3 other ways to flavour your couscous...

- **Walnuts with garlic and herb soft cheese** – swap the pine nuts for the same quantity of walnuts, and substitute the blue cheese with a dollop of punchy garlic and herb cream cheese (such as Boursin).

- **Pesto and mozzarella** – flavour the couscous with vegetable stock powder, then spoon a generous teaspoon of pesto (from a jar or home-made; see the recipe on page 37) in the base of each pepper before filling. Top with thick slices of mozzarella.

- **Spiced apricot and almond** – swap the dates for dried apricots, and the pine nuts for flaked almonds. Add a generous teaspoon each of cumin, coriander and turmeric. Leave out the cheese, but use a little extra butter on top.

Overnight pulled pork

I've often noticed that when I hold my hand over the campfire in the morning it's still lovely and toasty (providing it hasn't chucked it down!), so I wanted to find a recipe that would harness all the lovely gentle heat the fire gives off as it cools. This pulled pork is absolutely ideal as it cooks to perfection in the dying embers overnight. Stuff the tender tasty meat into soft baps for the most perfect Sunday brunch ever. After a long night around the campfire catching up with friends, this is just the ticket to revive you the morning after.

SERVES 6–8

5 tbsp tomato ketchup

2 tbsp soft brown sugar

4 tsp English or Dijon mustard

1 tbsp fennel seeds, roughly ground

2 tsp smoked paprika

2kg (prepared weight) pork shoulder, boned and rolled

3 large onions, thickly sliced

3 large carrots, roughly chopped

1 x 500ml bottle cider (doesn't need to be special; any type will do)

Sea salt and freshly ground black pepper

6–8 soft white baps, to serve

Assuming you have a cool box to keep the meat cold for a couple of days, the ideal low-fuss way is to marinate the meat at home and shove it in a ziplock food bag, so all you then have to do at the campsite is cook it.

In a small bowl, mix together the tomato ketchup, sugar, mustard, fennel seeds and smoked paprika. Rub this all over the pork, then seal it in a ziplock food bag before adding it to your cool box.

When you are ready to cook, line a Dutch oven with a triple layer of foil (to help make washing-up easier!) and scatter in the onions and carrots. Place the pork on top, season generously with salt and black pepper, then pour in the cider. Seal completely with a tight-fitting lid (add a layer of foil if your lid is a bit loose).

Place the Dutch oven directly on the dying embers of your fire, using a shovel to push the coals around the oven a little. Leave to cook overnight, about 12 hours is perfect (depending on the heat left in the fire). Have a peek inside the pot first thing in the morning to see how it's doing. If it's been a particularly cold or damp night, you may want to get the fire going again slowly to carry on the cooking process until brunch time. Like all fire cooking it's a bit suck-it-and-see, and with this dish the cooler the embers are, the better – you don't want the embers to be too hot and cook the pork too quickly.

To serve, tease the meat apart with two forks, pulling it off in pieces, and shove it into the baps. There may or may not be gravy to spoon on as well (depending on the heat of your fire and how much evaporation has occurred).

Caribbean salt-baked fish with sweet potato hash

Salt-baking fish is a brilliant way to keep it moist – the salt bakes to a hard crust as the fish steams gently inside. I use gilt head bream here, a fine and handsome fish with a large head and heavy bones (a 600g fish yields enough to feed a couple of people). If you use other fish, like sea bass or trout, a smaller fish would probably suffice.

As with many of the recipes in this book, preparation in advance is the key to simplicity. Everything can be chopped, mixed and bagged at home – it will all keep very happily for 2–3 days in a cool box.

SERVES ABOUT 4

For the salt-baked fish
1.5kg fine salt (cheap cooking salt is ideal)
1 Scotch bonnet chilli, deseeded and finely chopped (save a little for the hash)
2 tsp *each* garlic granules, dried thyme, ground allspice and freshly ground black pepper
125ml cold water
2 whole fish (about 400–600g each), gutted and scaled (such as gilt head bream, sea bass or trout)

For the sweet potato hash
1.2kg sweet potatoes, peeled and cut into 1–2cm cubes
2 onions, chopped
2 tbsp vegetable oil
A little Scotch bonnet chilli, reserved from the fish (optional)
1 vegetable stock cube, crumbled
Sea salt and freshly ground black pepper

You will also need a large, heavy-based frying pan or old roasting tin and a couple of sheets of foil to line it with.

For the fish, mix together the salt, chilli, garlic granules, thyme, allspice and black pepper in a food bag. In a separate food bag, mix together all the ingredients for the hash, then seal and pack.

When you are ready to cook, line the frying pan or roasting tin with a double layer of foil. Add the water to the bag of salt and spices and mix it about to make a rough paste. Spread half in the base of the lined pan or tin and lay the fish on top, then scatter over the rest of the salt mixture, pressing it down firmly.

Set the pan or tin on the grill over your fire (the heat should be reasonably gentle, certainly no flames) and leave to cook undisturbed for 20–35 minutes. The smaller the fish the shorter the cooking time. Test for doneness by piercing through the salt crust at the thickest part of the fish with a metal skewer. Leave for a few seconds, then touch the tip to your lip. If it is hot, the fish will be cooked.

Meanwhile, to make the hash, tip all the ready-prepared ingredients into an old fireproof (no plastic handles) saucepan or frying pan and set on the grill over the fire, frying for around 5 minutes until the onions are just starting to soften. Pour in a little water, just 5mm or so in the bottom of the pan, and cover with a lid or foil. Cook for about 15–20 minutes until the potatoes are tender, stirring once or twice, adding a little more water if it's looking a bit dry.

To serve the fish, break off the salt crust, pushing it to the side. Use a couple of forks to tease the top fillets away from both fish, putting the flesh on to a plate. Then grasp the tail and pull out and discard the spine from each fish – it should come away very easily with the head attached. Use the forks again to tease away the bottom fillets. Serve with the sweet potato hash.

Driftwood baked paella with samphire, chorizo, chicken and prawns

In Spain, genuine paella is cooked over an open wood fire and is always eaten outside. So I can't think of a more perfect celebratory dish to make on a beach camping trip. This version includes samphire and for me these thin green strands are the very essence of the sea and add a pleasing salty crunch. Replace with 2 handfuls of frozen peas if you prefer – just chuck them in a food bag when you leave home, where they will keep happily for a few days in a cool box.

I cook this dish over my fire pit using a combination of charcoal and foraged driftwood, with the tripod and grill hung over it.

SERVES 4

3 tbsp olive oil
3 red peppers, deseeded and roughly chopped
2 onions, roughly chopped
1 x 225g chorizo ring, sliced into 1cm discs
4 large chicken thighs, skin on and bones in
Large handful of cherry tomatoes, halved
3 cloves garlic, chopped
Generous pinch of saffron threads
Large glass of white wine (about 250ml)
1 chicken or vegetable stock cube

250g paella rice
500ml cold water
100g samphire
About 240g (prepared weight) raw king prawns, peeled
Sea salt and freshly ground black pepper

To serve
Small bunch of flat-leaf parsley, chopped
1 lemon, cut into wedges

Once your fire is ready, set a large (about 30cm), deep frying pan on the grill over the fire and add the oil, red peppers, onions and chorizo. Cook over a medium heat, stirring occasionally for about 20 minutes until the vegetables are starting to colour a little.

Part a hole in the vegetables and lay a chicken thigh in the gap, skin side down. Repeat with the other 3 chicken thighs, making sure the skin is in contact with the pan so that it colours nicely. Let them fry for another 20 minutes or so, shaking the pan gently from time to time to prevent sticking. By now the onions and peppers will be beautifully soft and the chicken crisp on the skin side.

Stir through the tomatoes, garlic and saffron, then fry for another 5 minutes or so until the tomatoes are collapsing. Pour in the wine and simmer for another 5 minutes, then crumble in the stock cube, stirring really well. Add the rice and season well with salt and black pepper, mixing thoroughly and turning the chicken thighs skin side up. Stir in the water, then push the rice under the liquid.

Cover the pan snugly with foil. Leave to simmer over the fire for about 25 minutes, giving the pan a little shake occasionally to check it's not sticking, but don't worry too much, a bit of stuck-on rice is the best part of a paella!

Remove the foil, scatter over the samphire and prawns, re-cover and let them cook in the steam for 10 minutes – when the prawns are pink all the way through they are done.

Scatter over the parsley and serve with lemon wedges to squeeze over.

best camping breakfasts

For me, breakfast is an essential part of the camping experience, where slow, lazy mornings often follow long, late evenings. I think the full works of bacon, sausages and eggs are essential at least once during any camping trip, but I doubt anyone needs a recipe for how to cook a classic fry-up their favourite way.

So here are a few other suggestions for memory-making breakfasts that will get your friends and family crawling out of their tents with grins on their faces. If I'm feeling like making a bit of extra effort, I'll get my fire pit going for breakfast and cook over that – a fireside breakfast is just as special as a dinner-time one. Otherwise, a camping gas stove is just as effective for all these recipes.

Fruity porridge

Normally I prefer a savoury start to the day, but just occasionally I crave something warm and sweet. Porridge, made with half milk and half water, fits the bill and it is an especially good way to begin a day that is a touch cold and damp. Once it has started to thicken in the pan I chuck in a handful of chopped dried fruit – apricots, prunes or dates are all great – to sweeten it. A pinch of ground mixed spice is nice too, stirred through as the porridge is cooking, as is a drizzle of honey over the top once it is spooned into bowls.

Garlic tomatoes with fried eggs

A speedy serving suggestion for 4 people, easily scaled down to serve 2 with a smaller pan.

Heat a little **olive oil** in a frying pan and add 2 big handfuls of halved **cherry tomatoes** and 2 thinly sliced cloves of **garlic**, then stir-fry over a medium heat for a couple of minutes until the tomatoes are softening. Season to taste with sea salt and freshly ground black pepper, then make spaces among the tomatoes, crack in 4–8 **eggs** (I usually allow a couple per person) and let them fry until cooked to your liking. Best eaten straight from the pan with crusty bread or pitta bread for dunking.

Fling-it-in frittata

Inspired by a bowlful of cold pasta from the night before, this could just as easily contain all manner of leftovers that are in need of a good home. The pasta makes up the carbohydrate element, just as potatoes do in a Spanish omelette. But sliced-up cooked potatoes or other vegetables, or cooked meat, can all be flung in, and the cheese can be whatever takes your fancy. If you have a camping stove with a grill you could use it to brown the top, otherwise the foil ensures the eggs cook all the way through.

SERVES 2 (GENEROUSLY)

2 tbsp olive oil
2 courgettes, sliced
3–4 tomatoes, roughly chopped
Bowlful of leftover cooked cold pasta (I used leftovers from the Pepper, Chorizo and Goat's Cheese recipe on page 114)

4 eggs
A few spoonfuls of cream cheese
Sea salt and freshly ground black pepper
Chilli sauce or tomato ketchup, to serve

Heat the oil in a frying pan, add the courgettes and fry over a medium heat for a few minutes until just starting to soften. Add the tomatoes and fry for another couple of minutes until they just lose their shape, then add the leftover pasta, or whatever other leftovers you might have, stirring over the heat until warmed through.

Reduce the heat to a minimum and crack in the eggs, stirring constantly to mix them up so they resemble an omelette (or you could whisk them in a bowl first, but I prefer to save on washing-up!). Season well with salt and black pepper, loosely cover the top of the pan with foil and leave to cook gently until nearly set, about 10 minutes.

When the frittata is nearly done, dollop on the cream cheese, then re-cover and finish cooking. Serve hot or warm with chilli sauce or ketchup.

Other good leftovers for the frittata treatment...

- A little chopped-up ham or salami
- Leftover cooked meat from the previous night's BBQ – chopped sausage or burger is a brilliant addition
- Replace the courgettes with mushrooms
- Use a few chopped-up sun-dried tomatoes in place of the fresh ones

Eggy bread with spicy fried mushrooms

Yes, you need two frying pans here, which is obviously double the washing-up, but it's so worth it – the combination of creamy eggy bread and punchy spiced mushrooms is a complete winner. I advise you to subscribe to the 'I cooked it, so you wash up' principle that rules in my house.

SERVES 2 (EASILY SCALED UP)

3 eggs

About 100ml milk (or single cream, if you prefer)

2 thick slices bread cut from a white loaf

3 tbsp olive oil

250g mixed fresh mushrooms (such as chestnut, button and oyster), torn into bite-size pieces

1 heaped tsp garam masala

A pinch of dried chilli flakes (optional)

1 clove garlic, crushed (optional)

Knob of butter

A little roughly chopped coriander

Squeeze of lemon juice, or to taste

Sea salt and freshly ground black pepper

A few rocket leaves, to serve (optional)

Break the eggs into a large mug and whisk together with the milk, seasoning well with salt and black pepper. Spread the bread out in a single layer in a couple of shallow bowls or use an old baking tin. Pour over the egg mix, then set aside until the bread has soaked up the liquid. This may take up to 30 minutes or so.

For the mushrooms, heat half of the oil in a frying pan set over a high heat. Add the mushrooms and fry for a few minutes without disturbing them too much so they develop a nice caramelized surface, then stir and keep frying until cooked, about 8 minutes in total. Add the garam masala, chilli flakes and garlic and fry for another minute. Remove from the heat, then add the butter, coriander and lemon juice. Keep warm whilst you finish the eggy bread.

Heat the remaining oil in another frying pan over a medium heat, add the slices of soaked bread and fry for a couple of minutes on each side until crisp and golden. Do this in two batches if necessary.

Serve the eggy bread with the mushrooms spooned over the top. A bit of rocket scattered on top adds another dimension if you have some.

For a sweet eggy bread...

Add a tablespoon or so of caster or granulated sugar to the egg and milk mixture, and soak the bread as above. If you have brioche or croissants in need of a good home (and you don't want to save them to make the bread and butter pudding on page 130!) you could use them instead of the sliced white bread; simply slice before soaking. I would fry the eggy bread in a little butter rather than olive oil. For a fruity topping, core and cut a couple of eating apples into wedges and fry in a little butter with a pinch of cinnamon and a sprinkle more sugar. If you don't want to do apples, a generous dollop of jam is also a good thing to top a sweet eggy bread with.

Flask drop scones with syrup and crushed summer berries

Drop scones, or Scotch pancakes, were an after-school treat when I was young but they make a perfect breakfast for hungry campers. In this recipe, the batter is made cocktail-style by shaking it up in a food flask. This not only means not much washing-up, but also that it's then all ready in its own cool vessel and easy to take down to the beach or wherever you want to light your fire. This is another recipe I get organized at home by weighing the dry ingredients (flour, sugar and baking powder) into a food bag and sealing, so it's less faff at the campsite. The berries, I find, are generally self-crushing – that's just what happens on the journey!

MAKES ABOUT 16 DROP SCONES, SERVING 4–6 PEOPLE FOR BREAKFAST, OR FOR A PUDDING OR SNACK

300g plain flour
2 tbsp caster sugar
2 tsp baking powder
4 eggs
250ml milk
Sunflower oil, for frying

To serve
Mixture of fresh summer berries (about 300g), packed into a tub
Golden or maple syrup (preferably in a squeezy bottle)

At home, weigh the flour and sugar into a ziplock food bag and add the baking powder. Shake it about to mix it up and seal tightly, squeezing out as much air as possible, then pack away with the rest of your food.

At the campsite, break the eggs into a large food flask and put the lid on tight. Give the flask a really good shake, up and down, back and forth, just as if you were making a cocktail. If your flask is one of those sensible unbreakable ones, this is a job that kids love to help with. Open the lid, pour in the milk and repeat the shaking; now it should be completely combined. Open the lid again and pour in the dry mix, before sealing and shaking well once more. Open it up just to check, the batter should be pretty smooth (the odd lump is no problem), but give it another shake if necessary. Seal up the flask until you are ready to cook – the batter will keep happily in the flask for a few hours.

When you are ready to cook, get your fire ready. I generally use my fire pit to cook these, but you could also easily use a camping stove.

Take a large frying pan, add a drizzle of oil and set on the grill over a medium-hot fire. When it's hot, give your flask a final shake, unscrew the lid and then pour in dollops of batter to make pancakes of around 10cm diameter. Cook for a couple of minutes (they are ready to turn when little bubbles appear on the surface) before flipping over with a spatula, then cook the other side for a minute or so. Serve immediately with crushed berries and syrup to taste, and repeat with the rest of the batter.

easy campsite puddings

Something warm and sweet when you're camping is a brilliant way to lift spirits that might be starting to flag, especially if it's getting a bit nippy or damp, so it's great to have a couple of easy pudding treats tucked up your sleeve.

Bread and butter pudding with marmalade and chocolate

The idea for this pudding was conceived at the end of a week of camping when we were left with a collection of slightly sad-looking leftover bits of this and that – a stale (and rather squashed) brioche loaf, half a jar of marmalade and two-thirds of a bar of dark chocolate, not to mention some just-on-the-turn milk. All in need of a good home, and what a home it turned out to be!

The beauty of brioche (croissants would be equally good too) is that they are butter-rich so you don't need to add any more butter. For extra richness, substitute some of the milk for a splash of cream (single or double), if you have some handy. Just as with the crumble on page 132, a foil-lined springform cake tin placed inside a Dutch oven is the best way to cook this recipe.

SERVES 6

1 brioche loaf (about 400g), torn into bite-
　size pieces
About ½ a jar of marmalade
About 70g dark chocolate, broken into bits

2–3 tbsp sugar (any sort is fine)
500ml milk
4 eggs

Line a 23–25cm springform cake tin with a double layer of foil. Scatter about half of the brioche pieces into the base of the prepared tin. Dollop on teaspoonfuls of marmalade, using about half of what you have, then scatter over about half of the chocolate pieces. Sprinkle on about 1 tablespoon of sugar. Repeat with the rest of the brioche, marmalade, chocolate and sugar.

In a bowl, lightly whisk together the milk and eggs, then pour evenly into the tin over the brioche layers. Place the tin inside the Dutch oven, cover with the lid and hang the oven over your fire, not too close to the coals otherwise the bottom will burn. Use tongs to put 8–10 hot coals on the lid to cook the pudding from the top as well. Cook for around 25–30 minutes until the custard has set and the top is crisp. Serve whilst piping hot.

Dutch oven apricot crumble

This recipe is an entirely ambient temperature crumble, using vegetable suet in place of butter and tinned fruit instead of fresh. I like to serve this with... you guessed it, tinned custard! When the sun has gone down and it gets a bit chilly around the campfire, you will get cheers of utter delight as you hand around bowls of this comforting pud.

SERVES 6 OR SO

200g self-raising flour
100g shredded vegetable suet
75g soft light brown sugar
50g porridge oats

1 tsp ground cinnamon
2 x 400g tins apricot halves in fruit juice
Tinned custard, to serve

This is best cooked in a springform cake tin that you place inside a Dutch oven. It simply means you can lift the tin out for easy serving and the foil-lined tin means the washing-up is minimal. So first line a 23–25cm springform cake tin with a double layer of foil, then pack it away until you are ready to cook.

Once again, get the dry ingredients ready at home. Weigh out the flour, suet and sugar into a ziplock food bag, then add the oats and cinnamon. Shake up the bag to mix everything together, then seal and pack away with your food.

When you are ready to cook, open up your tins of fruit and pour into the foil-lined tin, along with the juice. Turn the apricots so they sit in the tin, cut side up (so you have a nice dip in each half where the crumble settles). Shake up the bag of crumble topping to mix it again, then sprinkle over the fruit, spreading it evenly all over.

Put the tin into the Dutch oven and cover with the lid. Hang the oven over your fire, reasonably low over the coals to start with, and use tongs to put 8–10 hot coals on the lid to cook the crumble from the top as well (if it starts catching on the bottom, simply raise the oven up on the chain; use your nose to guide you – lift the lid a little and have a sniff). Cook for around 30–40 minutes, maybe a little longer, until the crumble is crisp on top. Serve whilst piping hot. I like to drizzle over cold custard straight from the tin but, of course, feel free to heat up your custard in a pan, if you prefer.

Other tinned fruit crumbles to try...

- Tinned gooseberries are great, although you may need to add a little extra sugar to the crumble topping as they can be quite tart. Replace the cinnamon with ground ginger.

- Pears in juice are delicious too. Add a handful of flaked almonds to the crumble topping, and replace the cinnamon with ground ginger.

- Tinned apple slices are brilliant with a little spice, so swap the cinnamon for ground mixed spice in the crumble topping.

Melty extra-chocolate muffins

A good way to quickly jazz-up shop-bought muffins. Take a **chocolate muffin** and pierce a hole in the top, twisting the knife to make a generous gap. Push in a chunk of your favourite **chocolate** so it's well into the middle of the muffin. Wrap it up in a couple of layers of foil and set in the glowing embers of your fire. After a few minutes, the muffin will be deliciously warm and the chocolate melted, and you will have forgotten you only opened a couple of packets to make it.

Sweet burritos

A wonderful thing for kids to make themselves – just put out a few options on the table and let them DIY their own pudding. Simply take a **soft wheat flour tortilla**, then fill and wrap it with pretty much any **sweet stuff** that takes your fancy. Roll it up tightly, wrap it in a generous piece of foil, then toast over the fire for a few minutes – either by laying it directly in the glowing embers, or on the grill.

A little parental warning – the contents of the burritos can get very hot, so let them cool a little before allowing kids to tuck in. Melted jam and marshmallows are particular culprits for mouth-burning.

Some favourite filling ideas…

- A tablespoon or two of your favourite jam, smeared all over the tortilla.
- What about jam *and* peanut butter for double the fun…?
- Chocolate chips, either on their own or spread with a base layer of jam – raspberry jam is perfect with dark chocolate; strawberry jam goes brill with white.
- Chopped-up tinned fruit, such as peaches, pears or apricots. A generous layer of nutella spread over the tortilla before you scatter the fruit will help it all stick.
- Mini marshmallows will melt into a sweet sticky heaven in moments.

Chocolate fudge bananas

Take a **banana** and peel a strip of the skin back. Make a slash down the centre of the banana and stuff in a **chocolate-coated fudge finger**. Lay the skin back over, then tightly wrap a sheet of foil around a few times, completely enclosing the banana. Lay in the glowing embers, or on the grill over your fire, and leave it to cook for a few minutes until the chocolate fudge has melted.

And if all else fails, there are always the ever-popular toasted marshmallows… See also Gingernut S'mores on page 96 in the Bonfire Celebrations chapter for a moreish marshmallowy treat.

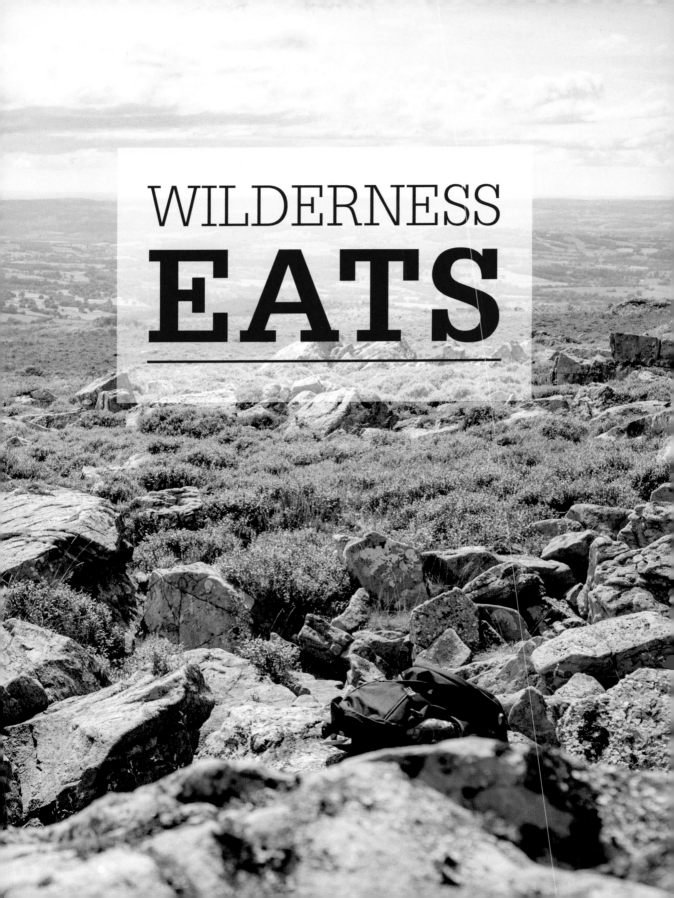

WILDERNESS
EATS

Introduction

In a perfect world, my ideal day would involve escaping the city at dawn and heading off to somewhere wild and windswept for a really long walk to clear cobwebs from body and soul. There is something enormously energizing about standing on top of a hill or cliff where the horizon is so big you simply can't take it all in. And as a greedy cook, for me no perfect day would be complete without something nice to eat, and the food I have eaten in wild places ranks high among my most memorable meals of all time.

At the moment, with two young children in tow, this kind of perfection is not reached quite often enough, but to maintain sanity I do need to escape from the rat race on a regular basis and I am trying hard to give my city-dwelling kids the sense of outdoor adventure I relished growing up. My early teenage years were spent yomping over Dartmoor as an air cadet, sustained only by Kendal mint cake and endless boil-in-the-bag slops in various shades of brown. I have no idea now what we were eating – a testament to their blandness that my memory fails me – but what I remember vividly was the sheer exhilaration of lighting up the stove and the pleasure of cooking something, anything, outside.

This chapter is all about minimal cooking for wild places (quite possibly in wild weather too!) and one-pan feasts that anyone can knock up on a single burner on a mountain side, including hearty, warming one-pot dishes and sustaining salads that are prepared in advance. And no walk in the wilderness would be complete without a few easy-to-carry treats to keep motivation up when spirits start flagging.

WILD COOKING EQUIPMENT

To cook in the wild you need a fairly compact and efficient cooker that you can shove into a rucksack, preferably one that is self-contained with its own pans.

My number one bit of kit is my Trangia stove, a single burner stove fuelled by methylated spirits. Also known as a 'storm cooker', it will let you cook in practically any weather, thanks to a wind baffle that protects the heat source from the elements. It comes with a couple of saucepans, a frying pan and a little kettle that all pack inside one another like Russian dolls. It is invaluable and I would rarely think of venturing into the hills without it.

As well as a cooker and pans to cook in, some sort of small spatula or lightweight wooden spoon is very useful for turning and stirring your food, as is a fork or a spoon with which to eat your hard-earned meal.

The other simply brilliant invention that was made for adventures is the food flask, perfect for transporting hot and ready-to-eat stews and soups, not to mention the ingenious 'pot noodles' on page 140. I like the individual serving-size flask as it means everyone has their own food to carry in their own rucksack, thus sharing the burden evenly. It also means you don't need to worry about taking serving bowls to eat out of, plus they usually contain a little fork or spoon tucked into the lid.

GETTING AHEAD – THE KEY TO A GOOD FEED

With these recipes you pretty much do all the work at home so that there is minimal faffing around in the wild. The other bonus is that many of these dishes are great for lunch and dinners at home too. So what I often do is make a big batch, then I have plenty to take with me on a wild adventure.

When I'm travelling with food that needs reheating, I usually pack it into individual portions in sturdy ziplock food bags. I then pop each one inside an enamel mug so they are protected from being spilt open as you walk.

EASY IDEAS WHEN YOU HAVEN'T COOKED AHEAD

With the best will in the world it's not always possible to get organized the night before, sometimes simply because the day has turned out to be more special than the weatherman thought and a spontaneous adventure is called for. Here are my favourite things for days just like that...

- **A tin of soup:** Tinned tomato soup was a favourite lunch of mine as a child, and it still hits the spot today, especially when you crumble a little bit of cheese over the top that melts slowly as you eat it. A recent holiday to North Yorkshire saw a morning dash to the corner shop for a couple of tins and a hunk of Wensleydale, which eaten nestled amongst the heather on top of a grouse moor made a lunch fit for a king.

- **Boiled eggs, again:** Just as with an impromptu picnic, hard-boiled eggs provide an endlessly useful travelling tucker option for when you're stomping in the hills. Neatly encased in their own protective shells, a couple of hard-boiled eggs per person, packed along with a little twist of salt and black pepper, make a very nutritious and sustaining lunch, especially when eaten with a bag of crisps for added crunch.

- **Something piggy:** You can't really go wrong with a bacon or sausage sandwich. To make life simple, get ahead just a little at home by taking the rashers or sausages out of their packaging and repacking them in a sturdy food bag, with a little drizzle of oil. Then all you need to do is get your frying pan nice and hot before sliding the contents of the bag in and cooking until crisp. I usually go one step further at home, slicing and buttering a few bread rolls, adding a squeeze of my favourite sauce and wrapping each in foil which then provides a reasonable sort of plate to eat off too.

AND FINALLY...

At risk of teaching you to suck eggs, don't forget to pack the cooker, pan and fuel too. Memorable for all the wrong reasons, a 15-mile walk on Dartmoor was recently completed with little more than a couple of ketchupy rolls between us when I packed the cooker but forgot the fuel. Not my finest hour. But it did mean that we'd really, *really* earned the cream tea at the end of the walk. Never has a scone tasted so fine.

better than a simple sarnie

Cheese, ham and pickle toasted sarnies

When you're halfway up a mountain or several hours into a country ramble, you want to be able to dig into your rucksack and pull out something sustaining and tasty. These toasted cheese and ham sarnies will both cheer you up and keep you fuelled in a way a standard sandwich will never do.

I use my portable Trangia stove, which is a super-handy bit of kit (see page 136). A little spatula is also useful to turn the sarnie over and lift it out, but with a bit of a deft juggle a fork would do!

Per person
2 slices bread (white, brown, seeded, whatever you like)
Softened butter, for spreading
Few slices of mature Cheddar cheese (about 60–70g)

1 slice ham
A little finely chopped onion, to taste (optional)
1 generous tsp or so of your favourite chutney or pickle

Tear off a generous sheet of foil and lay a slice of bread in the middle. Butter generously, then turn over and butter the other side. Lay on the cheese, then the ham and scatter over the onion, if using. Spread the chutney or pickle over the other slice of bread, then lay chutney-side down on to the filling. Butter the outside, then wrap tightly in the foil and pack away in your rucksack, along with a portable stove with which to fry it.

When you are ready to eat, fire up your portable stove. Get the frying pan nice and hot, then unwrap your sandwich and slide it in. Cook for a few minutes on each side until the bread is crisp and the cheese has started to melt. Use the foil you wrapped your sarnie in as a sort of plate and tuck in whilst still warm.

And for something different...

It's easy to adapt this sandwich, and here are a few of my favourite combos. The two important constants are the butter on the outside (this does the 'frying' bit) and the cheese. You can swap and change the type of cheese – just use something that melts nicely.

- Cheddar, tuna and roast pepper melt
- Mozzarella, salami and pesto
- Brie and cranberry sauce
- Stilton, grape and chopped walnuts

And for a pudding sarnie, what about a **Banana and Nutella toastie**? Spread Nutella on the insides of both slices of bread, adding a layer of sliced banana in the middle, then butter the outside.

Thai prawn pot noodles!

This hiker's lunch is so simple and so incredibly satisfying you'll wonder why you've never made it before. All you need is a food flask and something with which to boil a bit of water. And best of all, you can create an almost endless combination of flavours. I've listed a few of my faves below but I'm sure you'll come up with your own. The food flask keeps everything cool and insulated in transit so there are no worries about seafood or meat being unrefrigerated as you hike.

Per person
1 tsp soy sauce
½ tsp Thai red curry paste
1 nest fine (quick-cook) noodles (about 60g)
1 chestnut mushroom, finely chopped

1 spring onion, finely chopped
Finely chopped red chilli, to taste
Couple of sprigs of coriander, chopped
60g cooked peeled freshwater prawns
Sea salt and freshly ground black pepper

Get prepared at home before you leave. Add the soy sauce and Thai curry paste to the bottom of the food flask, then add the nest of noodles, snapping it up a bit to get it in if necessary. Follow with the mushroom, spring onion, chilli and coriander, just sprinkling them on top. Finally, scatter over the prawns and season to taste with a little salt and black pepper. Seal up your flask tight and pack away in your rucksack, along with a bottle of water for boiling.

When you've reached your lunch spot, boil some water, then pour it into your food flask. You need about 250ml (which in my food flask is two lots of the cup that sits on top of the flask). It might pay to measure the volume of your cup before you leave home. Turn the flask up and down a couple of times, then leave for about 10 minutes.

Give the flask another shake, then unseal and stir well to mix it up – the noodles should be cooked (if they are not, reseal and leave for a couple more minutes) and surrounded by a warming flavourful broth. Tuck in!

Other top pot noodle ideas...

Add these flavourings along with the noodles...

- **Curried chicken noodles** – add 1 teaspoon *each* of curry paste and mango chutney, 1 tablespoon finely chopped red onion, 1 tablespoon frozen peas, a little chopped coriander and around 60g shredded leftover roast chicken.

- **Beef, ginger and tomato** – add 1 teaspoon *each* of vegetable stock powder and soy sauce, 1cm piece finely grated fresh ginger, dried chilli flakes to taste, 60g shredded leftover roast beef and a few quartered cherry tomatoes.

- **Roast pork, sweetcorn and sweet chilli sauce** – add 1 teaspoon *each* of vegetable stock powder and soy sauce, 1–2 teaspoons sweet chilli sauce, 2 tablespoons sweetcorn, 1 sliced spring onion and 60g shredded leftover roast pork.

leftover magic

Spiced rice with fried eggs

I'm so thrilled with this easy way to use up a bowlful of leftover rice that it's now become one of my go-to quick lunches, whether I'm out walking or, far more boringly, at home chained to my desk. Eggs and spice were made for each other, and the rice gets a fabulous buttery crust on the bottom.

Rice safety is very important, so to keep it nicely chilled when I'm on the move I prep it straight into a food bag and pop it in the freezer overnight. Then it defrosts in my rucksack as I'm walking. After a couple of hours at ambient temperature it's ready to cook. If you want to eat it straight away or simply don't want to freeze it, pack the bag snugly against either an ice block or, even better, a frozen bottle of water that you can drink later.

SERVES 1 (GENEROUSLY)

About 200g cooked, chilled rice (white or brown, your choice)

Handful of frozen peas, about 75g (no need to defrost)

1 tsp of your favourite curry powder

A pinch of chilli powder (optional)

1 tsp olive oil

Small knob of butter (10–15g or so)

A little chopped coriander

A little sea salt and freshly ground black pepper

1–2 eggs

Spoonful or so of mango chutney to serve (optional), packed into a little tub

This is so easy. Simply take a food bag and add everything bar the eggs and chutney, giving it a shake-about to mix, then seal and freeze until you are ready to walk. Don't freeze it for more than a week to enjoy it at its best.

Pack the eggs (I normally opt for 2) into a small pot, tucking kitchen roll snugly around them so they don't break. Also pack a sheet of foil, folded up, that is big enough to cover your frying pan – this creates a lid for the pan, to speed up the egg-cooking process.

When you are ready to cook, fire up your portable stove and set the frying pan over the heat. Tip in the rice and pea mixture and stir-fry until piping hot throughout. Use a spatula or fork to push the rice aside to make a gap on the base of the pan. Crack in an egg (or two). Cover with the foil and cook the eggs to your liking. Eat straight from the pan whilst piping hot, dolloping on the mango chutney as you like.

Bubble and squeak-ish

An absolute 'leftovers' classic, bubble and squeak is one of my favourite things to cook on a hillside. And like all of my favourite things to cook, this one follows no hard and fast rules about ingredients – see below for plenty of ideas of how to ring the changes. Remember to pack your portable stove and frying pan.

SERVES 2

4 rashers streaky bacon, snipped into pieces
1 tbsp olive oil
500–600g cold cooked potatoes, crushed a little
Large handful of cooked cabbage/spring greens, shredded (about 100g raw weight)

25g butter
A pinch of cayenne pepper (optional)
75g mature Cheddar cheese, grated
Sea salt and freshly ground black pepper

You need 3 sealable sandwich bags for this easy recipe.

Put the bacon and oil into one sandwich bag and seal. Put the potatoes, cabbage, butter, cayenne pepper, if using, and a generous grind of salt and black pepper into another slightly bigger bag and seal. Add the cheese to the last bag and seal. Pack all three bags into your backpack, along with a small spatula or wooden spoon for stirring, and off you go (not forgetting a fork or two).

When you are ready to eat, fire up your portable stove and tip the oily bacon into the frying pan. Cook for as long as is necessary to get it slightly crisp, about 5 minutes on my stove.

Add the potato and cabbage mixture, stirring well to mix, and fry until hot and just getting tasty golden crispy bits on the potato, another 10 minutes or so on my stove. Finally, add the cheese and stir until just melting. Eat immediately – best straight out of the pan.

Some other easy ideas...

- Add some shredded cooked ham or leftover roast meat (beef, pork or lamb are all great) to the bag with the potatoes instead of taking raw bacon in a separate bag. Or how about a little diced chorizo for a bit of spice?

- Lose the meat altogether and add a handful of shredded smoked salmon – bag it separately and stir through just at the end of cooking to warm through.

- Ditch the Cheddar and replace it with something a little grander – Roquefort, Brie or aged Gouda are all great.

- Vary the veg – anything cooked will do, just have roughly equal amounts (by volume, not weight) of veg to potato.

- A bit of crumbled leftover stuffing in the mix is delicious!

three hearty home-made soups

These soups serve more than you'll probably need in one sitting, but they keep well in the fridge for up to 3 days and also freeze brilliantly for up to 3 months. Once cooked, simply cool, then pack into food bags or containers (as individual portions) and refrigerate or freeze, ready to take with you. You can then either reheat them at home and transport them hot in a food flask ready to eat on your travels, or you can pack them in your rucksack along with a portable stove, ready to heat through at your lunching spot.

Classic leek and potato soup

When it comes to eating, the classics are often the best, and this humble soup is both quick and delicious to make and very filling to boot.

SERVES 4–6

25g butter

2 tbsp olive oil

4 large leeks, washed and thinly sliced

3 large potatoes, cut into 1cm cubes

1 litre chicken or vegetable stock

2 tsp dried mixed herbs

Sea salt and freshly ground black pepper

Melt the butter with the oil in a large saucepan and sweat the leeks over a low heat for 5 minutes. Add the potatoes, pour in the stock and bring to a gentle simmer.

Stir through the herbs and season well with salt and black pepper, then cook, uncovered, for around 15–20 minutes until the vegetables are soft, stirring occasionally.

Use a wooden spoon to break up the potatoes a little for a rustic soup, or purée with a stick blender until smooth, if you prefer.

Cream of onion soup with rosemary

Anything creamy is comforting in my world, and this exceedingly simple soup is no exception.

SERVES 4–6

50g unsalted butter

750g onions, roughly chopped

1 tbsp rosemary leaves

2 tbsp plain flour

1 litre milk

salt and freshly ground black pepper

Melt the butter in a large saucepan and add the onions and rosemary leaves. Cover with a lid and cook over a low heat for 30 minutes, stirring occasionally, until the onions are very soft. Stir through the flour thoroughly, then pour in the milk, stirring constantly over a medium heat until the soup thickens. Remove from the heat and whizz until completely smooth using a stick blender. Season to taste with salt and freshly ground black pepper.

Double pea and pancetta soup

Bright green fresh pea soup would probably be my desert island soup dish. I love it both for its vibrancy and simplicity, but in this recipe I have used dried split peas along with the fresh to give a bit more filling sustenance. The pancetta can easily be left out for a vegetarian soup, but for meat-eaters it adds a great salty boost.

SERVES 4–6

1 tbsp vegetable oil
200g diced smoked pancetta or lardons
2 sticks celery, diced
1 large onion, chopped
2 cloves garlic, crushed

250g dried split peas (green or yellow)
1.5 litres vegetable stock
300g fresh or frozen peas
Splash of double cream (optional)
Sea salt and freshly ground black pepper

Heat the oil in a large saucepan, add the pancetta, celery and onion and sauté over a medium-low heat for around 15 minutes until the vegetables are soft.

Add the garlic and cook for a further minute, then stir through the split peas and pour in the stock. Bring to the boil and season with plenty of black pepper. Simmer gently, uncovered, for around 40 minutes until the split peas are soft. Stir in the fresh or frozen peas and simmer for a further 5 minutes.

Use a stick blender to purée the soup in the pan to a consistency you like (I like mine fairly smooth). Stir through the cream, if using, and add a little salt or more black pepper if necessary.

one-pot wonders

One-pot cooking is absolutely ideal for on-the-move food as everything you need comes in one neat ready-prepared package. These next few recipes can all be made ahead of time and taken chilled in a ziplock food bag packed into a mug or bowl, ready for reheating on your portable stove. Or you can reheat them at home and transport them steaming hot in a food flask for even speedier eating along your route. These recipes will all keep for up to 3 days in the fridge.

Two tasty ways with lentils...

Neat little parcels of energy and goodness, lentils have come a long way in recent years, shaking off their dull hippyish overcoat to become something of a vogue ingredient. I love them a myriad different ways, particularly the firm type, like Puy, or the large flat brown ones, that stay intact on cooking.

Here are two of my favourite ways with lentils, but both are ripe for tweaking so do experiment. Both recipes serve 2 but can easily be doubled to each serve 4. Once cooked, cool, then pack into food bags or containers and refrigerate, ready to take with you.

Chipolatas, red peppers and Puy lentils

I like to use thin chipolatas as you get more of the delicious caramelized crispy outside than with regular fat sausages but, of course, you can substitute those if you like.

SERVES 2

2 tbsp olive oil
6 chipolatas, each cut into 3 pieces
1 large onion, chopped
1 large red pepper, deseeded and chopped
A pinch of dried chilli flakes (optional)
125g Puy lentils

Handful of black olives
1 clove garlic, crushed
½ tsp dried oregano
500ml chicken stock
Sea salt and freshly ground black pepper

Heat the oil in a heavy-based saucepan set over a medium-high heat, add the chipolatas and fry for around 10 minutes until golden brown all over. Add the onion, red pepper and chilli flakes, if using, and fry for a further 10 minutes or so until starting to colour a little at the edges.

Stir through the lentils, olives, garlic and oregano, then pour in the stock and season well with black pepper. Bring to the boil, then cover and simmer steadily for around 40 minutes until the lentils are soft, stirring occasionally. Add a little salt and more black pepper if necessary.

Smoky aubergine and tomato lentils

Crème fraîche enriches this delicious vegetarian dish and elevates it firmly beyond 'worthy'!

SERVES 2

3 tbsp olive oil
1 large aubergine, cut into 2cm pieces
2 cloves garlic, crushed
½ tsp smoked paprika
4–5 ripe tomatoes, roughly chopped

1 tbsp balsamic vinegar
125g large brown lentils
500ml vegetable or chicken stock
1 heaped tbsp crème fraîche
Sea salt and freshly ground black pepper

Heat the oil in a saucepan over a medium-low heat, then fry the aubergine until softening and starting to colour, about 15–20 minutes. Add the garlic, smoked paprika, tomatoes and balsamic vinegar and fry for a further couple of minutes.

Stir through the lentils, pour in the stock and season with black pepper. Bring to the boil, then cover and simmer steadily for around 40 minutes until the lentils are soft, stirring every so often. Stir through the crème fraîche and season to taste with a little salt.

Lemony lamb and cannellini beans

Slow-cooked lamb and soft beans are sure to cheer you up mid-hike, but this stew is also a winner for the supper table too. It also freezes well for up to 3 months, so is a good one for batch cooking – enjoy half for your dinner and freeze the rest in portion-size food bags ready to take out on a wild adventure.

SERVES 4

2 tbsp olive oil
500g lamb neck fillet, cut into 2–3cm cubes
1 large onion, chopped
3 cloves garlic, crushed
3 sprigs of rosemary
2 x 400g tins cannellini beans, drained and rinsed

400ml vegetable, chicken or lamb stock
Large glass of white wine (about 250ml)
1 lemon
Small bunch of parsley, chopped
Sea salt and freshly ground black pepper

Heat the oil in a heavy-based saucepan over a high heat and quickly fry the lamb in a couple of batches until golden brown all over, transferring to a plate as you go. Reduce the heat a little, add the onion and sauté for 15 minutes or so until starting to caramelize at the edges.

Return the lamb to the pan, then add the garlic, rosemary and beans, stirring for a minute, before pouring in the stock and wine. Peel 2 or 3 wide strips of rind from the lemon using a vegetable peeler and throw them into the pan, then squeeze in the juice of half the lemon. Season well with salt and black pepper.

Bring to the boil, then reduce the heat; cover and simmer gently for around 1½ hours, stirring occasionally, until the lamb is really tender. Remove the lid towards the end of cooking to thicken the stock if you like.

Stir through the parsley and taste, adding an extra squeeze of lemon juice if desired. Cool, then pack into food bags or containers and refrigerate, ready to take with you.

And some more one-pot 'baked' beans

There's nothing wrong with tinned baked beans topped with a generous sprinkle of Cheddar (one of my go-to warming lunches when I'm working at home), but home-made bean recipes are in a different league altogether. In fact, these are not baked at all (nor, I suspect, are the ones in the tins), but they are perhaps the ultimate comfort food and just the ticket mid-hike.

Make at home the night before and take bagged and ready to reheat in a pan on your portable stove mid-walk. Or reheat at home and pour into a warmed food flask to carry them hot and ready to eat.

Butter beans, prosciutto, greens and Gorgonzola

SERVES 2 (RECIPE CAN EASILY BE DOUBLED TO SERVE 4)

2 tbsp olive oil
1 large onion, chopped
1 clove garlic, crushed
About 4 slices prosciutto, roughly chopped
1 head spring greens, shredded

1 x 400g tin butter beans, drained
   and rinsed
A little pinch of dried thyme
250ml vegetable or chicken stock
150g Gorgonzola, roughly diced
Sea salt and freshly ground black pepper

Add the oil and onion to a deep frying pan and cook gently for 15–20 minutes until lightly caramelized. Stir through the garlic and prosciutto and cook for a further couple of minutes, before adding the greens, butter beans and thyme, mixing well.

Pour in the stock and season with salt and black pepper, then bring to a simmer, cover and cook for 15 minutes until the greens are just cooked through. Stir through the cheese until it melts, then adjust the seasoning to taste. Cool, then pack into a food bag and refrigerate, ready for reheating the next day.

And another thing...

This is not so much a recipe but an idea to experiment with. From the recipe above, keep the gently caramelized onion (it adds much body and sweetness to the beans), and the garlic and stock. Everything else is very much a moveable affair, making it a great dish to use up bits and bobs of this and that...

- Swap the spring greens for green beans for a double-bean feast, or try a large handful of fresh or frozen peas. Add roughly chopped cherry tomatoes, or even sun-dried tomatoes for a richer taste.

- Replace the stock with an equal quantity of passata for a tomatoey dish.

- Change the beans. Cannellini beans go particularly well with tomatoes, and black-eye beans are great, especially if you add a pinch *each* of ground cumin and chilli powder (or dried chilli flakes) to the mix for a hint of Mexico.

- Use chopped bacon, chorizo or salami in place of the prosciutto. Or try it with some chopped sun-dried tomatoes and a few sliced black olives or capers.

- Replace the meat element with something salty and piquant, like chopped anchovies or capers.

- Try a different cheese – traditional Cheddar is great, especially with tomatoey beans.

- Change the herbs – try chopped coriander or parsley, added at the end of cooking.

- Spice it up with curry powder, chilli powder (or dried chilli flakes), cumin (ground or seeds) or smoked paprika.

a couple of sustaining salads

Salads are perhaps not your first choice for a filling and hearty lunch, but both of these tasty Mediterranean-inspired salads will keep you going for hours and are great for warm-weather adventures.

Pasta with feta, peppers and hazelnuts

SERVES 3–4

175g dried pasta (any shape you like)
50g whole unblanched hazelnuts
3 tbsp olive oil
2 red peppers, deseeded and chopped
1 clove garlic, crushed

200g feta cheese, crumbled
50g sun-dried tomatoes, chopped
A generous handful of flat-leaf parsley, chopped
Sea salt and freshly ground black pepper

Cook the pasta according to the packet instructions, then drain well.

Whilst the pasta is cooking, set a large frying pan over a high heat. Add the hazelnuts and toast for 2–3 minutes until they smell nutty. Tip on to a board and roughly chop. Set aside.

Add the oil to the frying pan and tip in the red peppers. Fry over a high heat, stirring from time to time, for 8–10 minutes until lightly charred at the edges.

Remove from the heat and stir through the garlic, then add to the cooked pasta (along with all the tasty oil), mixing well. Stir through the chopped nuts, feta, sun-dried tomatoes and parsley and season well with salt and black pepper. Spoon into containers and cool, then cover and chill in the fridge until you are ready to travel.

Couscous with tuna, chickpeas and halloumi

SERVES 3–4

150g couscous
200ml hot vegetable stock
3 tbsp olive oil, plus extra for frying
1 x 250g pack halloumi cheese, cut into 1cm slices
1 x 400g tin chickpeas, drained and rinsed

Finely grated zest and juice of 1 smallish orange
Handful of black olives
1 tbsp (drained) capers, roughly chopped
1 x 200g tin tuna (ideally in olive oil), drained
Sea salt and freshly ground black pepper

Add the couscous to a mixing bowl, pour over the hot stock, then cover with cling film and set aside for 10 minutes or so to allow the couscous to soak up the liquid.

Heat a griddle pan over a high heat until smoking hot, then lightly brush with a little oil. Fry the halloumi on both sides for a few minutes until crisp, then remove, chop into bite-size pieces and add to the couscous, fluffing lightly with a fork.

Stir through the chickpeas, orange zest and juice, the oil, the olives and capers, mixing well. Finally, lightly fork through the tuna and season with salt and black pepper. Pack into tubs, cover and chill in the fridge until ready to take with you.

something sweet and energizing

Sesame flapjacks

In my book, an old-fashioned flapjack should be just the right side of teeth-achingly crunchy, so these get a good baking, but cook them a little less if you like a softer bite. The sesame seeds not only add a lovely taste but are a nutritious superfood too, giving you masses of the good stuff wrapped up in neat little packages. These keep well for around 5 days in an airtight tin or wrapped in foil.

MAKES 12–18 PIECES

300g butter, plus extra for greasing
250g golden syrup
100g soft dark brown sugar

450g porridge oats
100g sesame seeds

Preheat the oven to 190°C/Gas 5. Grease and line a shallow 30 x 20cm baking tin with non-stick baking paper, leaving two 'tails' of paper overhanging to help lift the flapjacks out once baked.

Weigh the butter, syrup and sugar into a saucepan, then bring to a simmer over a medium heat, stirring well, until the butter melts and you have a smooth glossy sauce. Remove from the heat.

Combine the oats and sesame seeds in a large mixing bowl. Pour over the hot syrup sauce and stir thoroughly until evenly mixed. Scrape into the prepared tin, pressing down level with the back of a spoon.

Bake in the oven for 30 minutes until golden brown on top. Cool in the tin for a few minutes before slicing through into pieces, then leave to cool completely in the tin. Once cold, remove, wrap and pack up to take with you.

Or flavour your flapjack another way...

- If sesame seeds are not your thing, try swapping them for the same weight of different seeds or chopped nuts.

- Or you could try adding chopped dried cranberries, apricots, stoned dates or prunes.

- Add a little spice – a big pinch of ground cinnamon, ginger or mixed spice is ideal.

- If you're a fan of chocolate, you might like to drizzle over some melted chocolate as the bars are cooling, or how about adding a handful or so of chocolate chips to the mixture before you bake?

Orange and prune shortbread

Home-made shortbread is such a treat at any time, but eaten with a spectacular view in front of you and a mug of hot tea in your hand, it tastes mighty fine indeed. You can even freeze the uncooked mixture in the tin, well-wrapped, for up to 3 months, if you fancy making a double batch, then defrost before baking. Once baked, these keep well for around 5 days in an airtight tin or wrapped in foil.

MAKES ABOUT 12 PIECES

250g butter, softened, plus extra for greasing

100g caster sugar, plus a little extra for dusting

Finely grated zest of 1 large orange

250g plain flour

100g cornflour

200g dried stoned prunes, chopped

Grease and line a shallow 30 x 20cm baking tin with non-stick baking paper, leaving two 'tails' of paper overhanging to help lift the shortbread out once baked.

Add the butter, sugar and orange zest to a mixing bowl and beat together briskly with a wooden spoon until pale and a little fluffy. Sift over the flour and cornflour, then scatter in the prunes and stir really well until you have a crumbly dough. Tip the mixture into the prepared tin, pressing down firmly and evenly with the back of the spoon.

Cover with cling film and chill in the fridge for at least 30 minutes, or even overnight. This helps firm up the dough, giving you a crisper result on baking.

When you are ready to bake, preheat the oven to 190°C/Gas 5.

Bake the chilled shortbread in the oven for about 30 minutes until pale golden. Cool in the tin for a few minutes before cutting into about 12 pieces using a sharp knife, then leave to cool completely in the tin. Once cold, remove, wrap and pack up to take on your travels.

Other ideas to try...

- Leave out the prunes for a deliciously plain shortbread.

- Replace the prunes with other dried fruit – cranberries are a great sharp contrast to the sweetness, or try chopped dried apricots, stoned dates or dried apples.

- Add a teaspoon of caraway seeds for an interesting spicy flavour.

- Add a handful of chocolate chips when you sift in the flour.

Fruit and nut energy bars

With just a handful of ingredients, these speedy bars are absolutely packed full of energy and they are sure to give you a boost when you need it most. They are also a brilliant way to use up odd leftover nuts and seeds that you might have hanging around from past baking projects. These keep well for around a week in an airtight tin or wrapped in foil.

MAKES ABOUT 16 BARS (A LITTLE GOES A LONG WAY)

Butter, for greasing
250g honey (runny or set)
250g peanut butter (smooth or crunchy)
250g mixed nuts (like walnuts, almonds, cashews and brazils), roughly chopped

200g dried apricots, chopped
100g mixed seeds (such as pumpkin, sunflower and sesame)
100g desiccated coconut

Preheat the oven to 190°C/Gas 5. Grease a 25cm square cake tin with butter and line with non-stick baking paper.

Weigh the honey and peanut butter into a small saucepan. Melt over a medium-low heat, stirring from time to time, until you have a thick sauce. Remove from the heat.

Put the nuts, apricots, seeds and coconut into a mixing bowl. Pour in the honey and peanut sauce and stir thoroughly to combine, making sure everything is nicely coated and sticky. Scrape into the prepared tin, pressing down evenly with the back of a spoon.

Bake in the oven for 15–20 minutes until deep golden on top. Cool in the tin for a few minutes before cutting into squares, then leave to cool completely in the tin. Once cold, remove, wrap and pack up to take on your travels.

Index

159

ACKNOWLEDGEMENTS

Writing a book is just a part of its creation and I'd like to thank a whole host of people at Transworld Publishers who have been involved in making *How to Eat Outside* both beautiful and usable. Not least my lovely editor, Susanna Wadeson, and also Katrina Whone, Phil Lord, Alison Martin, Sarah Whittaker and Isobel Gillan. Big thanks one and all. Many thanks also to Anne Sheasby, who has done a brilliant job of copy-editing my text, especially as many of the recipes are cooked in an unconventional way, which I know presented a whole new level of challenges!

Thanks also to Kate Hordern, my agent, for loving and supporting the idea from the outset. And to another Kate … Kate Humble, for her enthusiastic support of the project from the beginning, and especially for agreeing to host a food and music festival to launch the book at her working farm, Humble by Nature.

Jason Ingram, not only a hugely talented photographer but also a friend with the patience of a saint, deserves my enduring thanks and quite possibly a medal too for the extra effort he put in to get such beautiful shots. I dragged Jason to all manner of wild and wonderful places and, whilst it was often challenging to say the least, we had a whole lot of laughs along the way.

And lastly, my lovely family and friends get an extra special big THANK YOU for their help in testing the recipes and joining in all manner of outside adventures. What a lovely fun-filled summer we had! I shall treasure it for years and years.

For Izaac and Eve, my very own little adventurers – I hope you will keep on finding fun in the small things even when you are big.

TRANSWORLD PUBLISHERS
61–63 Uxbridge Road, London W5 5SA
www.transworldbooks.co.uk

Transworld is part of the Penguin Random House group of companies whose addresses can be found at global.penguinrandomhouse.com

Penguin
Random House
UK

First published in Great Britain in 2015 by Bantam Press, an imprint of Transworld Publishers

Copyright © Genevieve Taylor 2015

Genevieve Taylor has asserted her right under the Copyright, Designs and Patents Act 1988 to be identified as the author of this work.

Photography: Jason Ingram
Food styling: Genevieve Taylor
Design: Isobel Gillan

A CIP catalogue record for this book is available from the British Library.

ISBN 9780593074510

Printed and bound in China

Penguin Random House is committed to a sustainable future for our business, our readers and our planet. This book is made from Forest Stewardship Council® certified paper.

1 3 5 7 9 10 8 6 4 2

MIX
Paper from
responsible sources
FSC® C018179